KU-185-488

THE VISITOR'S GUIDE TO
THE DORDOGNE

	Towns/Villages
	Motorways
	Mainroads
	Rivers
	Lakes/Reservoirs
	Railways
₼	Museum/Art Gallery/Centre
𝛑	Archaeological Site
	Castle/Fort
	Ecclesiastical Building
	Building/ Country Park
	Cave
	Zoo
✳	Other Place of Interest
	Nature Reserve – Safari Park
	Château

Visitor's Guide Series

This series of guide books gives, in each volume, the details and facts needed to make the most of a holiday in one of the tourist areas of Britain and Europe. Not only does the text describe the country-side, villages, and towns of each region, but there is also valuable information on where to go and what there is to see. Each book includes, where appropriate, stately homes, gardens and museums to visit, nature trails, archaeological sites, sporting events, steam railways, cycling, walking, sailing, fishing, country parks, useful addresses — everything to make your visit more worthwhile.

Other titles already published or planned include:
The Lake District (revised edition)
The Chilterns
The Cotswolds (revised edition)
North Wales
The Yorkshire Dales (revised edition)
Cornwall
Devon
East Anglia
Somerset and Dorset
Guernsey, Alderney and Sark
The Scottish Borders
    and Edinburgh
The Welsh Borders
Historic Places of Wales
The North York Moors, York and
    the Yorkshire Coast
Peak District (revised edition)
South and West Wales
Hampshire and the Isle of Wight
Kent
Sussex
Severn and Avon
Brittany (France)
Black Forest (W Germany)
The South of France
Tyrol (Austria)
Loire (France)
French Coast
Iceland
Florence and Tuscany (Italy)
Normandy

The Visitors Guide to

THE DORDOGNE

Neil Lands

MOORLAND PUBLISHING

HUNTER
PUBLISHING INC

British Library Cataloguing in Publication
Data

Lands, Neil
    The visitors guide to the Dordogne — 2nd
    ed.
    1. Dordogne (France) — Description and
    travel — Guide-books
    1. Title
    914.4'7204838   DC611.D7

Acknowledgemnets
Colour illustrations have been supplied by :
J. Dyer (Tursac, Les Eyzies); International
Photobank (Beynac, Pèrigueux, La Rocque
Gageac, Domme); H.M. Race (Rocamadour);
the remainder by the author. Black and white
illustrations have been supplied by: the
author pp 133, 135, 144; the remainder by the
French Government Tourist Office.

© Neil Lands 1986

Published by
Moorland Publishing Co Ltd,
8 Station Street,
Ashbourne, Derbyshire,
DE6 1DE England.
Tel: (0335) 44486

ISBN 0 86190 132 0 (paperback)
ISBN 0 86190 133 9 (hardback)

Published in the USA by
Hunter Publishing Inc,
300 Raritan Center Parkway,
CN94, Edison, NJ 08818

ISBN 0 935161 31 7 (paperback)

All rights reserved. No part of this
publication may be reproduced, stored
in a retrieval system, or transmitted in
any form or by any means, electronic,
mechanical, photocopying, recording or
otherwise, without prior permission of
Moorland Publishing Company Ltd.

Printed in the UK by
Butler and Tanner Ltd,
Frome, Somerset.

Contents

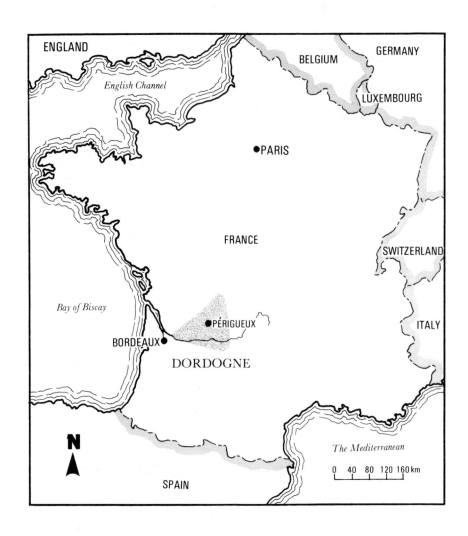

ENGLAND

English Channel

BELGIUM

GERMANY

LUXEMBOURG

●PARIS

FRANCE

SWITZERLAND

Bay of Biscay

●PÉRIGUEUX

ITALY

BORDEAUX●

DORDOGNE

N

The Mediterranean

0   40   80   120 160 km

SPAIN

1 An Historical Introduction

The Dordogne is a river in France. It rises in the Auvergne, near Mont Doré, flows south and west for some 300 miles, and marries briefly with the much larger Garonne to form the Gironde estuary and finally flows into the Atlantic at Bordeaux. One of the longest of French rivers and among the most picturesque, it flows through an immense variety of unspoilt country, constantly changing its nature, speed and direction, in a quest for the open sea.

The Dordogne is also an administrative region, or *département,* named — as many French *départements* are — from the principal local river. This *département* covers most of the former province of Périgord, to the east of the Atlantic coastline, and lies to the north of the valley of the Lot. The *département* is shaped like a rough diamond, the four corners reaching out towards Bordeaux in the west, Brive in the east, Montauban in the south, and Limoges in the north. Périgueux, the

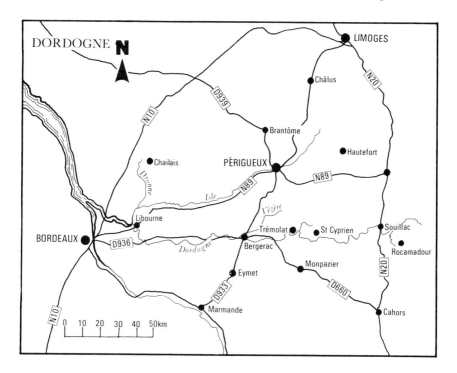

The Dordogne near Montfort

present capital, and once the capital of Périgord, lies almost in the centre of this region, some 300 miles (480km) south-west of Paris and 500 miles (800km) from the Channel coast at Calais.

Although the inhabitants of Périgord do not look on themselves as southerners, the Dordogne lies towards the south of France; Provence is not far away and the climate reflects the sunnier, milder aspects of southern France rather than the bleaker outlook of Normandy and the Pas de Calais, two regions probably more familiar to the British visitor or passing traveller, although the Dordogne has now become well-known and is a popular holiday region.

The climate of the Dordogne is soft and temperate, though tending to become very warm indeed in the summer when the oppressive heat is broken by spectacular hail storms and thunder storms. In the winter, snow lies on Mont Doré and the high peaks to the east, and can stay there until early spring; and in winter a good fire is needed, for the nights are chill. In the main, however, the Dordogne enjoys a fine climate, with long, golden summers which tourists from the colder north rightly envy and enjoy.

Snow on the hills almost suggests the Dordogne as a mountainous region. It may indeed seem so, with roads winding down the sides of sheer drops, and wooded hills reaching up to broad plateaux on every side. This is certainly the impression, but mountainous is hardly correct. The tallest peak in the area is only 630m (2,066ft) high, and while many peaks around the Massif Central and in the nearby Auvergne are certainly much higher, they lie outside the scope of this book. Rivers and their valleys are its main features and very beautiful they are. The Dordogne is divided into two main regions, Périgord Blanc, a limestone region around the *départemental* capital Périgueux, and Périgord Noir, a more wooded area spanning the Dordogne and Vézère valleys just west of Sarlat, at the foot of the small plateau, or *causse,* the Causse Martel, in the neighbouring antique province of Quercy. This is a very historic region which sprawls across the land east of the Dordogne from the Limousin region south to the Aveyron River.

This book is about Périgord, the modern *département* of Dordogne, and only incidentally about the river. There is enough history,

colour, scenery and interest in this star-shaped country to keep one occupied for a long time, let alone for a holiday, but short excursions may be made across the *départemental* border (if anything of great interest lies within reach), especially to see the *bastide* towns and the Cère and Maronne valleys.

Dordogne has not become a popular holiday region by accident. It is a microcosm of all that is best in France, with very few of the snags that come from extremes. It is warm in summer but the heat is not oppressive. It has great scenery but no barring mountains. It is still mercifully uncrowded, and if you shop around the prices are reasonable. Above all the Dordogne is beautiful and romantic.

I discovered the Dordogne some twenty years ago when making my way to Spain. Thousands of British tourists make the same journey every year, for the summer roads are usually full of GB-plated cars and caravans. In the last ten years Dordogne has become increasingly popular with the British, not only as a holiday area but also as a place to live. Many have homes in the valleys of the *département,* and they or their friends will rush south at the slightest opportunity, to the peaceful woods of the Dordogne.

It must be a labour of love to do so, for the Dordogne is not so easy to reach. The 500 mile journey from Calais is a steady two days' drive if one is not used to driving and wishes to arrive reasonably fresh, although the new and improving autoroute network helps enormously. One can, of course, fly to Bordeaux and hire a car, or cross to Cherbourg or Le Havre and drive down across Nor-

St Seurin Church, Bordeaux

mandy and part of Brittany; the Breton ports of Roscoff and St Malo too are very convenient. Whichever route is used, a car is necessary, in order to tour the unspoilt countryside and meet the charming people who live there. A more leisurely exploration may be made by cycle or on foot.

The Dordogne provides us with many prehistoric links: Neanderthal man and Cro-Magnon men lived in the area; and the painted cave at Lascaux, though now closed, is famous all over the world as a living example of prehistoric art, dating from some 17,000 years ago; there are many more such sites which many be visited.

Recorded history for this part of the world may be said to have begun when Julius Caesar invaded Gaul and after various campaigns defeated the Gallic chieftain, Vercingetorix, at Alesia in Burgundy in 52 BC. Roman rule was then applied to the new province of Gaul, and the pattern of development, the creation of towns, roads, and trade, with the introduction of Roman law, spread across the land, and lasted for centuries. As happened elsewhere in the Roman Empire, the customs of the conquerors were willingly adopted by the nobility among the conquered who, under Roman governors, administered the province to their own commercial advantage, and in many cases became Romanised to the point of taking Roman citizenship. Gaul was too large and diverse to be totally assimilated, and parts of the country, notably the Massif Central where the Dordogne rises, never became fully Romanised. The main tide of Roman culture flowed round this island of reaction and the main centres of Roman life were on the coast. Thus arose the *Provincia Romana,* which is now Provence, where at Nîmes, for example, the Maison Carrée and the Pont du Gard are among the finest examples anywhere outside Italy of the splendour that was Rome. In the Dordogne, Roman influence is less apparent and Roman remains are few, but the Romans gave the region as a whole a name that would endure. They called the region of rivers the Land of Waters, or *Aquitania,* which French retained as Aquitaine.

The Romans also brought Christianity to Gaul, and by the beginning of the fourth century the new religion was tolerated and Christian colonies were springing up everywhere. Among these early Christians was St Martin of Tours, one of France's most popular saints, and more relevant to our region, St Hilary of Poitiers. Rome, however, was now in decline and the legions, those bulwarks of her imperial power, were going home. In the third century, Teutonic Franks from the north and Alemans from across the Rhine invaded Gaul, and although they were initially driven off, the threat of further invasion continued to grow until in the fifth century the Visigoths, no plundering army but settlers, occupied Aquitaine, and then spread south into Provence. Their settlement and the final disintegration of Roman Gaul were hardly established when the Teutonic Franks, under Clovis, moved south to dominate the country and establish their rule over much of what would one day become France.

Clovis became a Christian in AD 496 and as a Christian king established the *regnum Francorum,* the kingdom of the Franks. His Merovingian dynasty collapsed at his death in AD 551, and for the next 200 years, what is now France was a land of petty, squabbling kingdoms, largely Christian in worship, but with little unity outside religion.

As so often happens, it was an outside threat which united the country, when in the eighth century, invading Saracens from Spain advanced across Aquitaine to their defeat by Charles Martel at Poitiers, in AD 732. Charles Martel's grandson united all the Christian kingdoms of the west into the Holy Roman Empire, and called himself Charles the Great or Charlemagne. Charlemagne ruled the Franks from AD 742 until his death in AD 814, but the empire died with him. Fresh barbarian invasions followed, notably that of the Northmen, who established themselves in Normandy; the descendants of Charlemagne ceased to rule the Franks by inheritance in AD 987, when the monarchy became elective. In that year the Franks elected Hugh Capet as their king, and his house ruled much of France until 1328, when the House of Valois came to the throne, an event which precipitated the Anglo-French conflict of the Hundred Years War.

The Hundred Years War, which is referred to constantly in the history of the Dordogne, formed only a part of a much longer conflict, and covers the period from the Battle of Crécy in 1346, which re-established the English as a power in France, to their defeat at Castillion in the Dordogne in 1453, an event which

led to their final expulsion. In fact the war lasted for over 300 years, and the story, which is full of fascinating complexities, has its roots in Aquitaine.

The French king can hardly have been pleased when William of Normandy won the crown of England in 1066, and became a king by right of conquest, owing nothing of his elevation to the King of the French, yet still owing the king homage as Duke of Normandy. There was however some slight advantage to the French in that the victory at Hastings moved the restless Norman court a good deal further away, from Caen to London.

However, barely a century later, when Henry Plantagenet, Count of Anjou, became not only master of the hereditary Angevin lands, but also King of England, Duke of Normandy, and, by right of his wife, Duke of Aquitaine, the French King then had a restless vassal who was in all but name an emperor, much mightier in economic power and military force than his overlord. Luckily for the French, the Angevins had within them the seeds of their own ruin in the form of their taste for family strife, and Henry II's great empire dwindled rapidly after his death until, in the early thirteenth century King John, whom the French call John Lackland, was driven from the last Angevin stronghold in Normandy.

Some years later, however, Louis IX, St Louis, gave back most of the Plantagenet lands to John's successor, Henry III, which was foolish, if saintly.

In the fourteenth century the French had dynastic problems, for King Philip V left only a daughter,

Château de Campagne

and women were prevented by the Salic law from inheriting the throne of France. Edward III of England claimed the title through his mother, daughter of Philip IV, but the French chose the late king's nephew Philip of Valois. Edward promptly invaded, and the Hundred Years War began. This ravaged France for over a century but it left the Dordogne with a great legacy of castles.

The Dordogne suffered much during the war and enjoyed a respite of no more than 100 years before the Wars of Religion broke out in France; the south again became a divided land, a battleground for opposing factions. The Dordogne was the great base for the Huguenots and their captains fought many battles there.

Henry of Navarre, the Protestant leader, had to become Catholic to possess his inheritance, the throne of France. If he did so he would lose his support among the Huguenots — but he managed it.

This is potted history, and a sketchy background to our story, yet it has to be told and understood if the peculiar history of Aquitaine and the people and places of the Dordogne are to be enjoyed in all their fascinating complexity. We shall return to this subject again and again in this book, and the reader should at this point realise that for much of French history the King of the French *(Rex Francorum)* was very far from being the King of France.

Hugh Capet ruled directly only in a small area around Paris, generally called the Ile-de-France, and parts of the north-east. His theoretical power, in the form of people who owed him allegiance, far exceeded his economic or military power. He was, at best, *primus inter pares*, and while his feudal power was great, it was equalled or exceeded by men who were, theoretically, his vassals. This said, it should not be imagined that the King of the French was ignored by his countrymen. Feudal bonds were no less real for being lightly worn, and the feudal lord would always try to keep his policies broadly in line with those of his sovereign — unless, of course, it suited him not to.

This, then, was the situation that prevailed with Hugh Capet in AD 987, and although his descendants pursued a policy of continuous expansion to bring more and more under their direct control, it was not until the time of Louis IX, St Louis, in the early thirteenth century that the major dukedoms and baronies of France were held by feudal right, and at the pleasure of the king, who expected homage from his vassals, and their support in war. This did not end the problem of rebellions which went on until the seventeenth century, but it formed a major part in making the King of the French into the King of France.

Within this broad framework, let us now look at Aquitaine, within the borders of which lies the Dordogne. During the reign of the Capets, the River Loire divided France into two very different countries. In the sunlit, tumultuous south, romance and chivalry blossomed in a way quite different from the rough-bluff manners of the north. Even the languages differed. The French 'yes' for example, was pronounced *oui* or *ouil* north of the Loire, and *oc* south of it, which gave to the south

the name of Langue d'oc. The Languedoc presented posterity with the idea of romantic love, which has caused considerable problems to the world ever since. They can hardly be blamed though, for their country was, and still is, a romantic place in which to live.

In this region Latin was the courtly tongue, and the *langue d'oc* the local patois. Educated men from north of the Loire could understand the *langue d'oc* but few could speak it. Within the Languedoc lay Aquitaine, one of the two great feudal dukedoms of the south, the other being Toulouse. Aquitaine comprised the counties of Poitou and Gascony, and disputed with Toulouse the lordships of Périgord and Auvergne. The Duke of Aquitaine and the Count of Toulouse were each as powerful as their overlord the King, and frequently at war with him, and with each other.

The people of Aquitaine were loyal, if turbulent, subjects of their Duke, fiercely independent, believing, then as now, that no good could ever come from a ruler north of the Loire. It was something of a shock, therefore, when their good Duke William IX died on pilgrimage in 1137, and his inheritance fell to his daughter, Eleanor, who was betrothed to the French King Louis VII, whom she promptly married. The Salic Law, which barred women from the throne, affected the royal inheritance. Eleanor was a fabulously wealthy heiress, apart from being very beautiful, and on their marriage Louis added her lands to his own.

The marriage, however, was not successful. Eleanor was too wilful

Château de Castelnau

for her husband, and he bored her to death. Worse, their only child was a daughter, again barred by Salic Law from the French throne. When she accompanied Louis on the Second Crusade, in 1147, Eleanor's determination to enjoy herself got the king's army into at least one Saracen ambush, and during their stay in Antioch there were rumours that Eleanor was having an affair with her uncle, the reigning Prince of Antioch, Raymond of Aquitaine. By now, relations between the king and his wife were at breaking point, and it was common knowledge that they no longer shared the same bed. This, clearly, was no way to provide France with an heir, and on their way home through Italy in 1149, the Pope himself took a hand in the matter, tucking up husband and wife in the same bed, with his blessing.

The result of this Papal intervention was, however, another daughter, and once again the marriage went into a decline. In 1151 Louis sued for divorce, on the grounds of consanguinity. He could have charged the queen with adultery, which would have led to her death, but Louis, if dull, was an honourable man, and there was no real proof against the queen. He even returned her dowry, the Duchy of Aquitaine, and by 1152 Eleanor was free. She had, however, to find another husband quickly, to lead her troops and defend her inheritance; so she offered herself to Henry Fitz-Empress, Count of Anjou and Duke of Normandy, who accepted the offer with alacrity.

Thus came to Aquitaine the most energetic of medieval rulers, who would have English kings among his descendants, and reputedly had the devil among his ancestors. The

English connection with Dordogne begins at this point.

Let us leave the history of the region for a while and return to the present. Périgord is, and always has been, an agricultural region. Over forty per cent of the area is forested, with a mixture of coniferous and deciduous trees. Timber and timber products are one of the major industries. The local woods also provide the region with fuel, for there is no coal in the Dordogne. The rearing of livestock, notably sheep, is becoming increasingly important.

On the Quercy plateaux, to the south-east, or the *causses* as these plateaux are called, sheep are kept in large flocks and reared for their wool, milk and cheese, as well as for mutton. The area around Bordeaux, along the Dordogne to St Émilion and beyond, is wine country, where broad reaches along the river are given over to the cultivation of the grape. For the rest, cattle, nuts (notably walnuts), are exported by the ton, and soft fruits, mostly peaches, plums, apricots and strawberries, are important in their season. Chestnut trees abound, and their fruit is a staple food for the feeding of livestock. The oak, which grows here in a feeble fashion, unlike the spreading giants once so familiar in English acres, nevertheless conceals among its roots that gem of French cuisine, the truffle. Truffles, which in nature resemble nothing so much as a lump of coke, are in fact the result of a fungus disease which afflicts the roots of young oaks. The Périgord farmer plants young oaks in close copses, thus restricting their growth in the hope that among the roots the truffle will flourish. To locate and extract this black gold, the locals employ trained dogs, the truffle-hounds, or, less frequently, a pig. Oaks over a certain size cease to produce truffles, and once they grow beyond this point they are ruthlessly chopped down. When shaved into thin flakes the truffle makes a feast of any dish, and is the essential ingredient in that speciality of Périgord, the pâté. Indeed, when a dish is described as being *à la Périgordienne* this usually means garnished with truffles.

Tourism has now become a major industry in the Dordogne and in the summer months of July and August the traveller may have some difficulty in finding accommodation in any town or village along the river. It is always advisable to find a room before five o'clock, or to book ahead, at this time of the year. Those who choose to camp will have no difficulty finding a pitch on excellent sites, especially if they travel outside the peak months. The weather will be fine at any time between April and October, and the welcome is always warm.

Along the upper reaches the Dordogne has been dammed, partly to prevent the water running off the land and being wasted, but mainly for the production of hydro-electricity. These dams are not unattractive, indeed the dam is probably modern man's most satisfying creation, and there is always some beauty in broad sheets of water. The dams have, however, transformed the river into a series of lakes, and above Argentat the character of the river has been totally changed.

Périgord is also a leading

The Clock gateway, Bordeaux

producer of tobacco, the rough leaf which, once cured, contributes to that pungent, unmistakeable odour one can find only in France; Bergerac is the main centre. Last, but not least, is wine. Bordeaux has had links with England through the wine trade at least since the tenth century. The reds of the region are justly famous, and the English palate cherishes the fine white wines from the grapes grown in the area between the Dordogne and the Garonne, in the region they call Entre-deux-mers, 'between two seas'. Within the Dordogne itself, St Émilion produces some fine clarets. Although for reasons of economy and profit, much of the fine wine is exported, the locals take good care to keep a share for themselves and their visitors. One can drink the local *vin ordinaire* very cheaply; it seems to be ambrosia and costs much more outside the region. Nevertheless, for a treat, the visitor should buy some of the great wines as well.

Near Bergerac, on the river, lies Monbazillac, which produces the favourite wine of the local people. Monbazillac is a sweet white wine, as are most of the white wines in the district, but the reds of Bergerac or the 'black' wine of Quercy, from Cahors, are also very drinkable. The dry whites of Duras are another favourite. The choice between red or white, sweet or dry, is limitless in this region of excellent wines.

The map will give the reader an idea of the Dordogne region, of the tilt of the land and the major cities and towns which surround it.

Within the boundaries of the *département,* there are no major cities, and Périgueux is by far the largest town, with a population of just over 50,000. Bordeaux is the largest city hereabouts, a major port, the centre of the wine trade and, since the end of World War II, a thriving centre for light and heavy industry of all types.

To the north lies Limoges, capital of the former province of Limousin and a fine city, once brutally sacked by the Black Prince, but famous today for the manufacture of beautiful and delicate porcelain. It was well known for its enamels in the thirteenth century.

To the south, beyond Cahors and the cathedral city of Albi, lies Toulouse, which like Bordeaux, has changed from being a quiet provincial city into a progressive, healthy, industrial town, but attractive. The French have a deft touch for modern architecture. They have the knack of blending old and new buildings into a pleasing whole, and a flair for design and style that the Anglo-Saxon, viewing the ruin of many beautiful English cities, can only envy.

Certainly the major surrounding towns of Toulouse, Bordeaux and Limoges, and many smaller centres in Dordogne proper, are even today pleasant places to visit, sensibly planned while still retaining that timeless air that comes only from cities of considerable antiquity. The smaller towns and valleys of the Dordogne are very pleasing to the eye, and blend in beautifully with the natural splendour of the country. Geologically, Périgord leans to the west and is formed from a limestone plateau, pushed up and then tilted sideways by the upheaval of the Massif Central many millions of years ago. It is, in fact, one vast plateau and the rivers which seam the country have, over the years, cut deep wooded valleys in the limestone, slowing and widening as they run further west. It was the action of these rivers, some running on the surface, others flowing deep underground, which tunnelled out the deep caves and grottoes of the Dordogne region, home of the primitive hunters who painted the walls at Lascaux and Les Eyzies, and the basis for a branch of archaeology, the study of prehistoric man.

These caves also gave refuge, in the Middle Ages, to the local people, terrorised and dispossessed by the raiding armies of England and France, and the mercenary free companies of men-at-arms, who lived by pillage between campaigns. Some of the caves have been converted into pleasant dwellings that people still live in today, but others have become attractions for the growing number of tourists who visit the Dordogne each summer. Most notable of these attractions is the underground monolithic abbey of St Émilion, which has been hacked out of the limestone rock. Le Grand Roc cave at Les Eyzies, on the Vézère, is always crowded, but well worth a visit: so is Padirac in Quercy, just outside the *département*.

The sprawling Dordogne country, seamed by the rivers and ravines between the higher *causses* or plateaux, can only be explored with any facility by car. The roads are very good, if a little narrow and very winding, as they climb up the valley sides to the higher viewpoints. Everywhere, glorious views open up before the traveller, and a temptation not to be resisted is to stop and gaze at the beauty of the scene. In the fine weather which the region enjoys from spring to late autumn, the traveller can see for miles in the clear, unpolluted air. Only when the fierce 'Atun' blows, that stinging hot wind which can scorch a face not used to it, does the air become unpleasant. For the rest, the Dordogne is a land of delights.

2 The Road to The Dordogne

You do not need a car to get to the Dordogne, for you can fly or go by train. There are direct flights from London and New York to Bordeaux, and the rail network is very fast and very good. Some form of transport is certainly necessary, though, if you are to see much of the country when you arrive. Besides,

France is one of the few countries left where motoring is still a pleasure. Even the minor roads have the speed of a motorway without the monotony, and perhaps more important, without the congestion which you find on those winding English roads. The traveller to the Dordogne area has a choice of

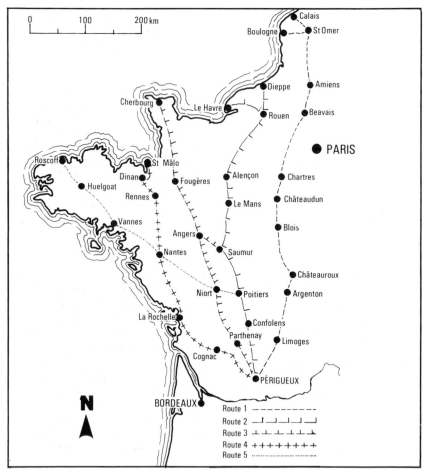

These routes are not exactly
direct, and the linking sections
should be made on minor roads
wherever possible, but all are
worth seeing. The 'red' Michelin
maps Nos 998 and 999, are best
for planning these routes. In high
season (mid-July to end August)
overnight accommodation should
be booked ahead, or found before
6pm.

route, each taking about the same
time but offering a variety of
attractions *en route.*

The short sea route from Dover to
Calais or Boulogne takes a little over
an hour, and leads the traveller
through St Omer and Arras, on to
the Paris road, and so south. This is
the road of World War I, with Vimy
Ridge looming up on the left before
Arras, and the shattered quiet of the
Somme battlefield lying to the right
of Bapaume, on the road south to
Paris which, needless to say, offers a
wide choice of attractions. The road
from Dieppe heads across some of
the most beautiful countryside in
Normandy, and has the advantage
of offering a wide choice of
secondary roads to the traveller who
likes to wander, and passes, for
example, Chartres, where the
cathedral alone is worth a day of
anyone's time. The motorway
network is now almost complete,
but the Dordogne-bound traveller

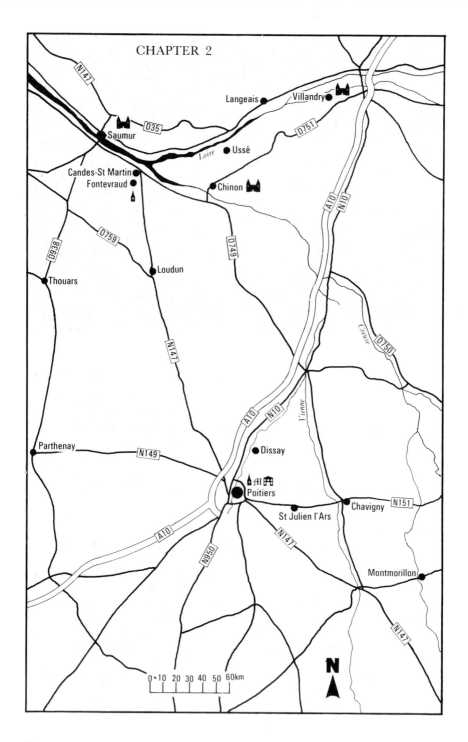

CHAPTER 2

N147

Langeais · · Villandry

D35

Saumur

Loire · Ussé

D751

Candes-St Martin ·
Fontevraud ·

· Chinon

D759

D938

· Loudun

D749

· Thouars

N147

A10 N10

Creuse D750

A10 N10

Vienne

Parthenay ·

N149

· Dissay

· Poitiers

· St Julien l'Ars

· Chavigny

N151

A10

N950

N147

Montmorillon ·

N147

0 10 20 30 40 50 60km

N

Angers

---

inevitably ends up in either Limoges or Poitiers.

Perhaps the best route south leads from Cherbourg. It is possible to cross over by night from Southampton and arrive at the French port in the morning in time for an early start, but occasionally one can (or must) leave the boat much earlier than the official time for docking. At Carentan, just inland, the Auberge Normand is one of the nicest inns in Normandy, where not an eyelid is flickered at a disgruntled, unshaven Englishman marching in at 7am demanding hot water and coffee. It may well be wise to book a room for the return trip. Right beside the Auberge lies a most interesting military museum, dedicated to the 101st US Airborne Division, which captured Carentan

from the Germans in 1944. It has an excellent collection of weapons, uniforms, and equipment. Not far from Carentan, at Ste Mère Eglise, where the 101's sister division, the 82nd, landed, is another museum, and a magnificent church in the main square.

From Paris, perhaps the best route is thorough Chartres and Limoges. There are connecting flights direct to La Rochelle and Bordeaux, and the route south takes one past Coutances, with its fine Gothic cathedral, and Laval in a long sweep down to Angers on the Loire. Angers is relevant to our story, for it was for generations the ancestral home of the Angevin Counts of Anjou, who ruled in the Dordogne after Henry II married Eleanor, and one of their ancestors, Fulke,

managed to get himself related to the Devil.

It appears that a long time ago, Count Fulke went away on a journey and returned after some years married to a beautiful lady. They seemed very happy and in the course of time had four children, two boys and two girls. Two things about his wife puzzled the count. Firstly, she appeared to have no relatives, and in an age when everyone of a certain class knew everyone else, her lack of kin seemed a little odd. Secondly, she seemed very reluctant to attend Mass which, with the constant Feast days and setting an example to the lower orders, took up a lot of the nobility's time. The lady always managed to avoid Mass, until one day the count very unwisely decided to make an issue of it. When she next entered the church he made two of his largest knights stand on the hem of her cloak. All went well until the bell tinkled for the elevation of the Host, at which point the lady began to scream in agony and, tearing herself loose from the cloak she seized two of her children and flew out of the window! Neither she nor the children were ever seen again and her husband, not surprisingly, went into a decline and soon died.

It transpired that his wife was Melusine, the Devil's daughter, and from her two remaining children by the count all the later Counts of Anjou were descended. When Count

Geoffrey, father of Henry II of England, reigned in Angers, the story of his descent from the Devil was known everywhere, even if few intelligent people believed it. The Angevins were a ferocious family and far from ashamed of their devilish origins.

Geoffrey has another claim to fame, for like all medieval kings he was a great hunter and loved all aspects of the chase, particularly hawking. To improve the cover for birds, he used to carry with him cuttings of gorse and broom which he would plant in any likely spot; this habit earned him a curious nickname which remained with his line for nearly 400 years. His followers called him the 'Broom-Planter' or *Plant-a-genet,* 'genêt' being the French word for gorse or broom. Count Geoffrey was a mild and honourable man, and when he died at the early age of thirty-nine, he left to his son Henry a contented and prosperous country.

In the twelfth century Anjou was, in itself, one of the great feudal countries of France, but Count Geoffrey had also inherited from his mother the adjoining county of Maine, and he married Matilda, daughter of Henry I, King of England. By marrying her he became King of England and Duke of Normandy. However, Geoffrey had few territorial ambitions and had no great love for his wife. Besides, on the death of Henry I the

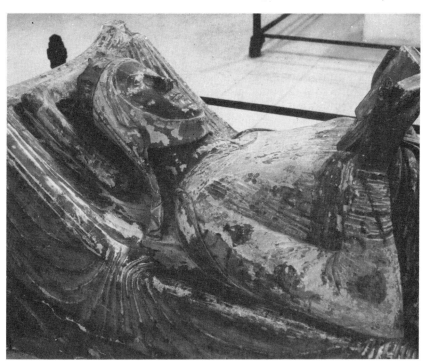

Effigy of Eleanor of Aquitaine, Fontevraud

Abbey kitchens, Fontevraud

English elected Stephen to the throne, and a cruel war between Stephen and Matilda raged in England for twenty years, during which time, as a chronicler put it, 'God and his Saints slept'. Geoffrey wanted no part of these brawls, and ruled his counties and the Duchy of Normandy as an inheritance for his son, Henry, born in 1133. This was the Henry who was later to marry the beautiful and wilful Eleanor of Aquitaine, and become Henry II of England.

Angers lies on the River Maine, a tributary of the Loire. The road south crosses the Loire just south of Angers and then forks left towards Saumur. This is one of the great garrison towns of France, famous

Cathedral of Notre Dame, Poitiers

down the ages as a cavalry centre, and home today of that splendid equestrian team, the *Cadre Noir*. The town has a very enjoyable feature today, for this is the place to stop and enjoy the very delectable dry white wine which comes from the lower Loire, Muscadet.

SIGHTS WORTH SEEING IN THE
LOIRE VALLEY INCLUDE:

The Château-Fort, Chinon
Open: 9am-12 noon and 2-7pm.

**The Plantagenet Mausoleum,
Fontevraud Abbey**
Open: 9am-12 noon and 2-6.30pm.

**The Château of Chenonceaux,
south of Blois**
Open: 9am-7pm.

The town of Amboise.

**The Muscadet vineyards around
Nantes.**

**The Gardens, Château of
Villandry**
Open: 9am-12 noon and 2pm-
sunset.

Most wines take their name from the district or vineyard where they are grown, but Muscadet takes its name from the grape itself, a plump, white, juicy, fruit which grows along the valley, and makes a remarkably fine wine. It is drunk throughout France, but especially in Brittany and Normandy where it complements the excellent seafood for which those provinces are famous.

The Loire flows through Saumur, and once across the river we enter old Languedoc. Nowadays, that once great area has shrunk in name to a single region on the Mediterranean coast, but when the Plantagenets ruled, the whole area south of the Loire reflected an air and an attitude much warmer and more volatile than the lands to the north. To the south of the Loire, the weather always seems to become warmer and the difference between France and England becomes more noticeable.

Henry II died at the castle at Chinon on the Loire, alone and brokenhearted, after the defection of his youngest son, John. His body, dressed in borrowed finery, was brought twenty miles to Fontevraud, mausoleum of the Angevin dynasty.

The religious order of Fontevraud was established in 1101 and in the twelfth century the abbey there contained a monastery and a nunnery. Indeed, the superior was an abbess. Henry II once considered sending his son John to be a monk there, for John was always interested in religious matters and he might, had things turned out differently, have become a very good archbishop instead of a remarkably bad king.

The abbey became a favourite foundation of the Angevin gamily and was frequently in receipt of gifts, usually made to atone for their latest crime. At all events, the abbey prospered. Henry II was buried there in 1189, and Richard Coeur-de-Lion joined him ten years later, to be followed by his mother, Eleanor, who returned to Fontevraud in her old age and died there in 1204. The abbey has suffered the usual damage, both from age and the depredations of fanatics, serving after the Revolution as a barracks and a prison, but it has been beautifully restored, and is well worth a visit.

The effigies of Eleanor, Henry, Richard and Isabel (John's wife) are kept in the abbey church. These effigies are particularly interesting because they still carry much of their original paint, and are quite handsomely coloured. Nowadays we are used to simple whitewashed churches, relieved perhaps with oak, brass, and some stained glass. The medieval churches were not like that at all. They glowed with colour, with rich frescoes on the walls, bright brasses and the tombs of the local nobility and gentry, and altar cloths glowing below the cross. Much goodwill was stored up for the next world by decorating God's house in this. The colourful effigies of the Angevins are just a brief reminder of the splendour that has gone. It is strange to look at them now, for those effigies at Fontevraud are the sole remains of a family which once ruled most of Western Europe, and whose quarrels shook empires.

The Angevin family and their descendants, the Plantagenets, ruled England and, intermittently, much of France, from 1133 until 1485. In the end, torn apart by their own quarrels and hunted down relentlessly by the usurping Tudors, their line was totally extinguished and all their energy and power drained away. In the seventeenth century a judge summed up their fate when giving a verdict in a suit over the also defunct Earldom of Oxford:

> Where is Bohun? Where is Mowbray? There must be a period and a stop to all temporal things, an end to names and territories, and whatsoever is terrain. Where now is Bohun? Where too is Mowbray? Nay, last and most of all, where is Plantagenet? They are entombed in the urns and sepulchres of brief mortality.

From Fontevraud the road leads down to Poitiers, a great city and once capital of the Duchy of Aquitaine. Modern Poitiers is a healthy industrial city, with large factories and office buildings standing around the town. It was near here, in 1356, that Edward of Woodstock, later known as the Black Prince, fought a French army which barred his route to Bordeaux, and crushed it utterly, taking prisoner the French King, John the Good, and most of the surviving knights and barons.

The Prince had been on a *chevauchée,* a great plundering raid across France, when the French army overtook him near Poitiers. Laden with booty which they were reluctant to abandon, the English troops took up a defensive position, in their usual harrow formation, with men-at-arms in the middle and the fearsome archers on the flanks. Remembering the chaos the English bowmen had caused the mounted French cavalry at Crécy eleven years before, John dismounted his main divisions or 'battles', and led them on foot against the English line. This was a disastrous mistake, for it is one thing to stand and fight in full armour and quite another to march half a mile in it, under an arrow storm. Moreover, the prince had kept a force of mounted knights under the Gascon captain, the Captal de Buch, who charged the French from the flank, and routed them, the French king and his son Philip being taken prisoner by the English.

'The Black Prince' is a curious

nickname. No one called him that during his lifetime and the first noticeable reference to it is in Shakespeare's *Henry V*, where the French king, on hearing of Henry's landing, says:

> ... he is bred out of that bloody strain, that haunted us in our familiar paths,
> When Cressy battle fatally was struck,
> And all our princes captive by the hand of that black name,
> Edward, Black Prince of Wales.

Which although not accurate, makes the point.

Some claim that the prince wore black armour, which is unlikely; others that the name arose from the gloom and despondency he spread among his enemies, which is perhaps more credible. The most probable explanation, however, is that black was his favourite colour. The Prince of Wales' crest, which was adopted from that of Bohemia after Crécy, had three white feathers on a black field, and it is recorded that when the prince brought the captured King John into London, he rode beside him on a black pony, while the king rode, as was proper, a white warhorse.

At Poitiers the traveller has two main choices, either to go south via Lussac and Limoges, or take the western route through Angoulême. The latter is probably faster, for it is now a dual carriageway or autoroute, along which the products of Poitiers are taken down to the great port of Bordeaux. It also leads the traveller through the Cognac country, which no lover of brandy would readily miss.

Another route is via Lussac-les-Châteaux, on the River Vienne, which brings one into the Dordogne by a historic series of landmarks.

By the bridge at Lussac, on the Poitiers to Limoges road, lies an inn where the sign bears an interesting heraldic device. *Argent, a pile gules:* a strange device, resembling a red wedge on a white background, which no-one would know today, but in the fourteenth century there was not a knight in Christendom who would not recognise the blazonry of Chandos. One-eyed John Chandos, Constable of Aquitaine, friend and tutor of the Black Prince, was the most famous knight of his day, and his exploits were a source of song and story during his lifetime and for years after his death. He fought in all the wars of Edward III and the Black Prince. He was at Nájera when the Prince took an army into Spain to help Pedro the Cruel overthrow his half-brother, Henry of Trastamare, and gained nothing from it but the great ruby which glows today in the English Imperial State Crown, and the recurrent dysentery which was to wreck his health and temper, and finally kill him.

During the Prince's long illness, John Chandos led the armies of Aquitaine against the ever bolder invasions of the French, who had themselves found an inspired leader in Bertrand de Guesclin. It was a war of ambush and flight, with no great battles, but many minor skirmishes, and in one of these, by the bridge at Lussac, John Chandos was killed, stabbed through the visor on his blind side. Even his enemies, the French, mourned his passing, and helped to bury him in a little mound near the place where he was killed. His sarcophagus is up the little road behind the inn. Later on, a monument was erected and it still stands there today. That and an inn sign are the only memories remaining of one who, in his time, was the most famous knight in Christendom.

France is a country which cannot be rushed. It is twice the size of Britain, but with the same population, which gives it large empty spaces and merciful amounts of peace and quiet. As this chapter will have indicated, the road to the Dordogne should be part of the holiday, not simply a tiresome journey, and should not be hurried. From any of the entry towns in Picardy, Normandy, Brittany, or Paris, it is possible to select a route which can take in fine towns, ancient monuments and good food.

3 Into The Dordogne

Following the route described in the previous chapter to Bellac, 25 miles (40km) from the city of Limoges, the traveller stands on the doorstep of the Dordogne and inside the Limousin plateau.

This region, like the Dordogne itself, is farming country, with little industry other than that connected with the land. Most of the farming is pastoral, mainly cattle-rearing for beef, and the fields which border the roads are full of stock, usually the light brown cattle of France, with only the occasional herd of Frisian milkers. Sheep are here in abundance, rather smaller than those in the English South Down flocks, and reared mainly for their wool.

The fields are bordered by deep woods, while as one moves south and the rise and fall of the land becomes more pronounced, whole hillsides are given over to forestry. Happily, most of the trees are deciduous — oak, ash, birch and beech — and their variety makes the woods a beautiful sight, avoiding the monotony of evergreen coniferous plantations. Timber is another of these rural industries, and logging operations are apparent everywhere, the roads spattered with heavy mud from the wheels of the tractors.

Bellac itself is a small pleasant town overlooking the valley of the Vincou, the town rising up in a series of layers from the floor of the valley, and topped by a magnificent late Romanesque church. From the south, the views of Bellac across the green valley are very beautiful, while inside the town, quiet, narrow streets wind up and down, and give deep and welcome shade on a hot day. Bellac was the birthplace, in 1882, of the playwright Jean Giraudoux. A curious sight is the Hôtel de Ville, once the town's castle, which retains many thirteenth- and sixteenth-century features, including watchtowers on the walls. Small gardens and a weekly market add to the charm of the town which is a good centre for touring the Limousin.

Bellac lies on one of the main roads south, and on summer weekends, especially during July and August, endures some formidable traffic congestion. It is one of the pleasures of France that if one leaves the main roads, the smaller ones are just as fast and frequently deserted; so from Bellac, side roads lead to the village of Oradour-sur-Glane.

The Limousin plain seems much flatter than it actually is, for the wooded hills conceal the valleys, and level out the undulations of the land-scape, which is already taking on some aspects of the warmer south. Even stumpy palms can occasionally be seen growing in a sheltered spot. Wild flowers flourish, as tall purple foxgloves edge the roads, and daisies speckle the fields among the browsing cattle.

The road runs along the tops of the ridges and rises steadily, raised

Périgueux

Hautefort

Château Monbazillac

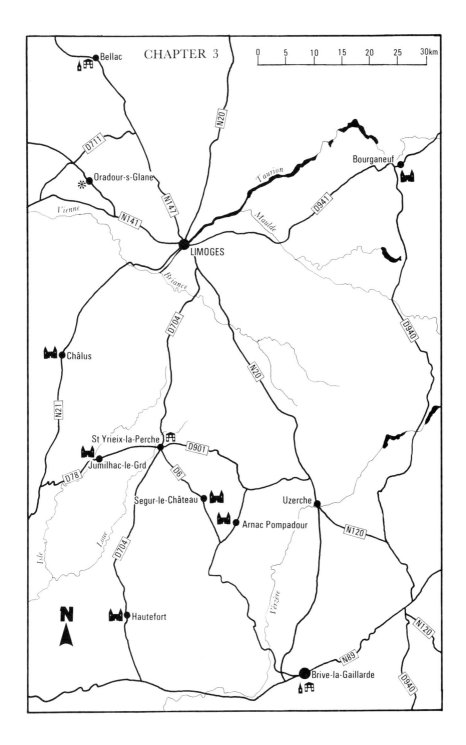

CHAPTER 3

Bellac

0 5 10 15 20 25 30km

N20

D711

Taurion

Bourganeuf

Oradour-s-Glane

D941

Vienne

N141

N147

Maulde

LIMOGES

Briance

D704

D940

Châlus

N20

N21

St Yrieix-la-Perche

D901

Jumilhac-le-Grd

D6

D78

Segur-le-Château

Uzerche

Arnac Pompadour

N120

D704

Loue

Isle

Vézère

N

Hautefort

N120

N89

Brive-la-Gaillarde

D940

PLACES TO VISIT IN THE
LIMOUSIN

Bellac
Birthplace of Jean Giraudoux
(1882-1944) and a fine Gothic
church. Also Hôtel de Ville which
used to be the town's castle

The Cirque de Peyrat
A rocky escarpment on the River
Vincou, near Bellac, with views to
the hills around Blond.

Châteauponsac
A pretty village on the D49 and
D711, east of Bellac. Church of St
Thyrse, Benedictine priory and
fifteenth-century houses.

Blonde
Twelfth-century fortified church.

Oradour-sur-Glane
Old village remains of destruction
by the German SS in 1944.

The Monts de Blonde
South of Bellac, a rocky wooded
area at around 500m (1,500ft),
with good walking from Blonde,
south to Beaucartie.

Peyrelade
South-west of Blonde, with fine
views over the Limousin plateau.

Limoges
Capital of the Limousin, on the
River Vienne. See the Gothic
cathedral of St Etienne (St
Stephen). See Museum of
Limousin Folklore (open: daily
except Tuesday, 9am-12 noon
and 2.30-5.30pm), also Musée
Adrien Debouche, contains a
collection of 10,000 pieces of
Limousin ceramics and porcelain
(open every day except Tuesday,
10am-12 noon and 1.30-5pm).

up far above the land with fine views
on either side. The upper reaches of
the Dordogne river have been
dammed in several places as a source
of hydro-electricity and the cables
take the power away to the factories
of the north, for the Dordogne river
provides France with a significant
amount of the energy she needs.

The little village of Blonde, which
lies on the cross-country road 10
miles from Oradour, has a fine
example of a fortified church. These
churches are by no means
uncommon in this part of France,
but the one at Blonde is a
particularly fine example. The
church dates from the twelfth
century, and was fortified in the
sixteenth century, probably during
the Wars of Religion. The presence
of these fortified churches gives
some indication of the warfare
which raged across this land for
centuries, and reached a terrible
climax in World War II at Oradour.

The French have been very clever
and successful in reconstructing
their towns and valleys after the
ravages of war, particularly in
Normandy; over 5,000 towns and
villages were totally destroyed there
in World War II, yet the houses have
been so well rebuilt that they look as
if they have stood for centuries. This
is not so at the new village of

Town Hall, Bellac

Oradour-sur-Glane, where the houses still look painfully new, and the whole village overlooks the ruin of the old. George Santayana once said that a nation which forgets its history is doomed to relive it. If true that alone is a good enough reason for visiting Oradour, which was the scene of one of the most bloody massacres in history, and one which took place not in the Dark Ages, but within living memory.

On the afternoon of 10 June 1944, troops of the German 2nd SS Division (Das Reich) surrounded Oradour. When the Allies landed on D-Day the division had been refitting in the South of France and was hurried north to join the fighting round the Normandy beaches. All the way north they were harassed, ambushed, and sniped at by the *Maquis* fighters of the French Resistance, and near Oradour two of their outriders had been killed. The divisional commander therefore decided to carry out a reprisal.

They rounded up the entire population of Oradour and paraded them in the main square. When they had separated the men from the women and children, the killing began. The men were machine-gunned and only three managed to escape. The women and children were locked in the church, which was then set alight, and the whole village was put to the torch. This was no 'reprisal', but wholesale murder. The Germans killed 642 people; over 200 of them children. They shot the village priest and both the doctors, and old Marthe, who was over seventy years of age, and little Mayre, who was only six. They shot her sisters, too.

The SS left, and Oradour's terrible story leaked out to the world. A low wall now surrounds the village, and has been left as the local people found it when rescuers began to reach the village after the SS had departed. The main street runs between the roofless houses, many with charred shutters still swinging in the windows. Inside, one can see the twisted remains of family possessions, a sewing machine, the treadle buckled by the heat of the fire, a bicycle, rusting on a wall, a car still parked in a garage. The railway lines still run down the street, and the wind sighs quietly in the telephone wires. Inside the church the altar still stands, though bullet marks pock the stones. Oradour is a sad and yet strangely beautiful place, and even the visitors seem subdued. It can hardly be the happiest place to visit on holiday, but if one needs a reminder to urge the unity of nations, this is it.

From Oradour the road south follows the valley of the Vienne. It is a wide and pleasant river, and we follow it on the road between Limoges and Périgueux, as far as the village of Aixe, where we turn south for Châlus. It is also possible to proceed through Limoges, the capital of the Limousin, but Limoges is a big city where traffic jams are certain, so veer off at this point and head to the east to Bourganeuf, which is a pleasant town with a curious story and a very good small hotel, the Commerce, in the Rue Verdun, where the food is excellent and most reasonable in price.

Bourganeuf was the home and prison of the Turkish Prince, Djem, at the end of the fifteenth century. Djem, or as the French prefer to call him, *Zim-Zim,* was the brother of the Turkish Sultan, Bayezid II. Djem had rebelled unsuccessfully against his brother, and, on the collapse of his revolt, had fled, for fear of the bowstring which awaited him in Constantinople, and taken shelter with the Knights of St John of Jerusalem, the Military Order then based in Rhodes.

The Order was organised into companies called *Langues,* and it was the Langue of Auvergne which took the prince into custody and transferred him to their castle of Bourganeuf, where he lived in considerable splendour, while his brother, the sultan, happily paid the knights 40,000 ducats a year to keep him prisoner. In 1489 Djem and his ransom were transferred to the custody of the Pope, Innocent VIII. He became a familiar figure in Rome and lived in great comfort in the Vatican.

Fate, however, had not finished with Djem. In 1494 the French king, Charles VIII, invaded Italy. Charles was more than a little mad, and his intention was to annex the kingdom of Naples and use it as a base for a Crusade against the Turk. On his way through Rome, Charles demanded the surrender of Djem from the Borgia Pope, Alexander VI, intending to use the prince during his crusade, and Alexander had no option but to hand him over. The sultan had offered a considerable sum to ensure that his brother took no part in the French king's crusade, and before handing the prince over, Alexander administered a poison to him. Or so the legend has it. In fact Djem did not die until a month after he left Rome, and then probably of the plague. One wonders what thoughts Djem must have had during these long years in captivity, passed as he was like a parcel from one hand to another, to die at last, alone among the Infidel.

Châlus is another of these little hilltop towns, dominated by a castle. But this castle at Châlus is of particular interest to the English because it was here that Eleanor of Aquitaine's third and favourite son, Richard Coeur-de-Lion, King of England, was mortally wounded, on 6 April 1199.

The Lord of Châlus had found a hoard of treasure buried on his land, but refused to share it with his liege lord, Richard, who took a party of *routiers,* under their captain, Mercadier, to demand it. While reconnoitring the walls, the king was struck in the shoulder by a crossbow bolt and died a few days later of blood poisoning. He was forty-three.

Mercadier took the castle before the king died, and the man who had fired the fatal arrow was brought before the king, to plead for mercy. Richard forgave him and ordered Mercadier to set him free, but after Richard died the *routier* captain took the archer to Eleanor. She had no mercy for the man who had killed her son, and had the archer skinned alive!

There is very little left now of the castle of Châlus, except for some of the bailey walls and an enormous tower from which wonderful views can be obtained over the little town and the surrounding countryside.

Leaving Châlus, one goes south again, via Ladignac to see the great castle of Jumilhac-le-Grand. The *ac* endings are very common hereabouts and are said to date back

---

PLACES TO VISIT IN AND NEAR CHÂLUS

Château of Montbrun
Spectacular moated castle on D64, six miles west of Châlus, built in the twelfth century and modified in the fifteenth century. Richard Coeur de Lion beseiged it without success.

Le Puyconnieux
Pretty village near Montbrun, with fine views from the hills nearby.

Forest of Boubon
Perfect picnic spot, an oak wood near Montbrun on D22.

Châlus Castle
Richard Coeur-de-Lion, King of England, mortally wounded here, 6 April 1199.

Castle of Jumilhac-le-Grand
Begun in the thirteenth century with usual Périgordien cupolas.

to Roman times, being derived from
their word *aqua,* water. Water is
such a feature of the Dordogne area
that it is not surprising to find it
attached to place names. Passing
through the country the traveller
will quickly notice the many small
artificial lakes or ponds which are
sprinkled across the landscape. The
region has an adequate rainfall, but
the rain runs quickly off the land,
and there would be problems for the
stock in high summer without these
little lakes to store the water. They
also seem to contribute to the
French countryman's great love, *la
pêche,* for most have a boat on them,
or are fringed with fishermen at
weekends. Another natural feature,
apart from ponds, are walnut trees.
Nuts of all types, but particularly
walnuts, are a speciality of the
region, and the best Périgord dishes
are either flavoured with truffle or
cooked in walnut oil; either singly or
in little groups, the walnut tree is a
common sight, and few fields seem
to be without one.

The castle of Jumilhac-le-Grand
stands on a hill above the River Isle,
a river which runs down through
Périgueux, and eventually into the
Dordogne at Libourne. At Jumilhac
the river is no more than 50 yards
wide and slow moving, winding
round the cliff on which the castle
stands. The castle itself is
spectacular, a huge building
crowned with the usual Périgordien
cupolas. It was begun in the
thirteenth century but added to
continually for the next three
centuries, until it reached the
massive proportions it retains today.

From Jumilhac, the road south-
east leads to the village of Angoisse,
where for those who like good food

Château de Pompadour, Corrèze

in a quiet and charming setting,
Chez Marcel in the central square is
not to be missed. The quiet in these
Dordogne farming villages is one of
their great attractions, especially
around midday, when many of the
villages seem quite deserted while
the inhabitants presumably give
themselves over to the pleasures of
the table.

At Angoisse one turns east, out of
the Dordogne *département* for a
while and into the neighbouring
département of Corrèze, to the castle
of Pompadour.

The beautiful and desirable
Marquise de Pompadour, mistress

of Louis XV, never actually visited Pompadour, let alone lived there: she would have found it much too dull and provincial. In spite of this, the town has done very well in the last 200 years from her name and reputation, but since she did well for herself as Madame de Pompadour, this seems only fair.

Jeanne, Marquise de Pompadour, was born plain Antoinette Poisson, in 1721, and first met her royal lover in 1745. She was the daughter of a municipal clerk. Her father was caught in some unlawful speculation and was forced to flee abroad, and during his absence her mother became the mistress of Norman de Tournhem, who educated her children and married Jeanne to his nephew. Jeanne was instructed in all the social graces and found her way into the then fashionable *salons* of Madame Deffand and Madame Geoffrin. She attended a masque at Versailles, at which, by some chance, both she and the king wore the same costume, being disguised, of all things, as yew trees. They therefore had plenty to talk about and very little to do, and within a few months Jeanne became Louis' chief mistress and Marquise de Pompadour. She was elegant, witty, and very popular, even with Louis' wife.

'If we must have mistresses', said the Queen, 'I am glad we have Madame de Pompadour.' The Pompadour is better remembered for her patronage of the arts, and it was under her influence that Paris became the artistic capital of Europe. The porcelain factory of Sèvres was started at her instigation, and she was instrumental in directing work to the tapestry trade of Gobelin and Aubusson. She also protected the writer Diderot and the members of his circle, then engaged in compiling their enormous *Encyclopaedia*. Madame Pompadour was an intelligent woman who saw quite clearly what would happen unless the Ancien Régime changed its ways and gave more freedom to the people, but '*Après moi le déluge*' is her best remembered aphorism.

She was the king's mistress for five years, and his firm friend for twenty more; yet it is recorded that, when she died in 1746 and her body was removed from Versailles, Louis watched from a balcony without a sign of regret. He did, however, establish a stud farm at Pompadour, which is now the National Stud for Arab horses, and this alone of his institutions still remains in being. The castle at Pompadour forms part of the stud, and can be visited on most days.

Near Pompadour, and well worth a detour, is the little village of Ségur-le-Château, home of the Comtes de Ségur, who were leading soldiers and courtiers at Versailles during the reigns of Louis XV and XVI, and later, Napoleon. One Comte de Ségur who became Marshal of France and Minister of War to Louis XVI, placed such value on blue blood as a source of military ability that he decreed that no man could be an officer in the French army unless his coat of arms displayed four quarterings of the nobility. What Napoleon would have made of that is anyone's guess, for his only requirement in a general, apart from ability, was that he should be lucky.

Ségur is also the ancestral home of the d'Albrets, who became Kings of Navarre and France. The castle stands above the river which encircles this quaint village, and an hour here would make a pleasant diversion.

Pompadour and the Corrèze *département* are pleasant places, well used to tourists. The next village is the delightfully named St Bonnet, and the road then turns west towards Hautefort, across the valleys of various small rivers. This reminds us yet again that we are on a plateau, or rather a series of plateaux, none particularly flat on top and all well wooded, but they are there because the rivers have carved out valleys below the level of the land and not because the land is particularly mountainous. From St Bonnet via the little town of Badefols-d'Ans, we approach Hautefort. Badefols has a wonderful martial castle, a real *château-fort* with machicolated walls and a roofed keep, standing, as usual, on a hilltop. It dominates the surrounding countryside, and glares across the valley at the rival towers of Hautefort.

Hautefort was devastated by fire in 1968 and has only recently been repaired, but for size, setting and splendour, not less than for a long, curious history, the château at Hautefort is unique in Périgord. One is prepared for the size since the castle dominates the surrounding countryside from whichever direction one approaches, but its outstanding beauty is a surprise. The setting itself, above the little town, is superb, and, closer to the walls, the castle rises up, with lawns beneath the battlements and with beautiful, well kept gardens along the terrace of the castle below the towers. Hautefort has everything, a park, a drawbridge across a dry moat, a knot-garden and a wonderful arboured walk before the gate. A huge forecourt of carefully raked gravel sets off grey-yellow walls which sparkle in the sunlight. A delightful spot!

On the site of the present château

stood, in the twelfth century, the castle of Bertrand de Born, 'the friend and enemy of kings', and in his way a real character. Bertrand was a powerful baron, a troubadour and a trouble-maker. He had charm, talent, and not a single moral scruple. His particular genius lay in keeping the Angevin family at each other's throats, though this could not have been a very difficult task, by composing *sirvantes,* or political songs. He was, in modern terms, a satirist.

Bertrand's problem lay in the fact that his father had left the lands and castle at Hautefort jointly to his two sons, Bertrand and Constantine. Since each wished to oust the other, Constantine swore loyalty to the Old King, Henry II, while Bertrand approached anyone who would support him, usually one of Henry's sons. He managed to rouse the young King Henry against his father, and indeed with his silver tongue kept everything in a satisfactory state of turmoil for years. The only one he failed to influence was Richard Coeur-de-Lion, whom he nicknamed in a *sirvante* 'Richard Yea-and-Nay', but with the rest of the Angevin family he was more successful.

As any modern satirist knows, a state of turmoil is necessary for success, for if the State is at peace and contented, all influence is gone. Bertrand's influence on the young King Henry kept the latter either at war with his brother Richard, or in rebellion against his father. Richard, who was no man's fool, knew where the root cause of the trouble lay, and when young Henry died in 1183, still in rebellion against his father, Richard took his knights to

---

PLACES TO VISIT FROM POMPADOUR

Ségur-le-Château
Medieval village dominated by ruins of great twelfth-century castle. To visit the castle apply at the gate.

St Yrieix la Perche
Old towns, famous for the production of Limoges clay. Fine old houses, much medieval architecture. The church contains the reliquary of St Yrieix.

Coussac-Bonneval
In the middle of a park supposedly designed by Le Nôtre, the late medieval château of Bonneval (fourteenth to fifteenth century). Open: Wednesday and Sunday afternoons only.

Castle of Hautefort
Seventeenth-century château, on medieval foundations. Restored 1969.

Hautefort Château

Hautefort and drove Bertrand out, putting the more amenable Constantine in his place. It was no good though; Bertrand went and begged forgiveness of the old King Henry, who, still grief-stricken over the death of his heir, gave Bertrand back his castle. Later in life, Bertrand left Hautefort and entered a monastery, where he eventually died. In the later Middle Ages Bertrand gained increasing notoriety, comparable almost with that accredited to Machiavelli.

Dante, in particular, thought Bertrand to be a fiend, and included him in Hell in his Divine Comedy.

Colourful Hautefort, now being carefully restored, is a wonderful place to visit, quite apart from the history of Bertrand; and one can only hope that when the restoration is complete, all the former splendour will return.

From Hautefort our way lies to the south-east, across the hills again to the far corner of the Dordogne and the town of Brive-la-Gaillarde, at the meeting place of the roads from Limoges to Toulouse and Bordeaux to Clermont-Ferrand. It is

therefore a traffic nightmare and
best visited by the passing tourist on
a Sunday, when at least the
commercial traffic is not so heavy.
Brive is really quite pleasant, and
certainly worth a visit, if only to eat
at La Crémaillère in the Avenue de
Paris.

The suffix, la Gaillarde, means the
'gay' or 'saucy' city, and is a tribute
to the citizens' staunch defence of
their town during various sieges. It
was once fortified and the boulevard
which encircles the old quarter
around the church of St Martin
follows the line of the walls. St
Martin's has been over-restored, but

PLACES TO VISIT FROM BRIVE LA GAILLARDE

Brive is a great centre for the
surrounding countryside, full of
attractions and well worth
exploring.

The Corrèze Valley
This runs to the north-east of the
town, in the Limousin. Visit
Autazines and go on foot to Puy
de Pauliac for marvellous views.

Roche de Vic (638m)
Take the N680 east from Brive.
This must be climbed on foot, but
it is a short round walk of about
half-an-hour.

Tulle
This town was once famous for the
manufacture of lacy veils, hence
'tulle'. It has an excellent
restaurant, La Toque Blanc, in
the Rue Jean Jaurès. A pleasant
half-day excursion.

Uzerche
Uzerche lies in the Limousin, to the
east of Pompadour, and is a small
but beautiful town on the Vézère
river. The rail trip from Brive to
Uzerche is very entertaining as the
track runs along the Saillant
gorges.

there are some interesting old houses
nearby, notably the Tour des
Echevins, or Aldermen's Tower. The
town has plenty of hotels and is a
good place to stay for a day or so, as
a centre for a detour into the
Corrèze valley which runs away to
the east.

4 Périgueux and Périgord Blanc

The road from Brive to Périgueux runs for much of its length along the valley of the River Vézère, which flows south from St Bonnet and then turns to the west for a while through Terrasson-la-Villedieu, before it turns south again towards Les Eyzies.

Terrasson is a quaint place where two bridges cross the river, and it marks the boundary between the Limousin region and the old province of Quercy. The road to Périgueux crosses to the north bank of the Vézère by the modern road bridge, from which there is a good view of the narrow, much more gracious, medieval bridge, built in the twelfth century, wide enough only for pack animals. Terrasson is the place to buy truffles, and there is a good local wine.

From here the route passes through Rastignac which has, or rather had, a magnificent château, the style of which was supposed to have inspired the architecture of the White House in Washington. In 1944 the château was set alight by the Germans, as a reprisal for Maquis activity in the area, and is only now being restored.

At St Laurent, on the right-hand side of the road to Périgueux, lies

Weir on the Dordogne at Bergerac

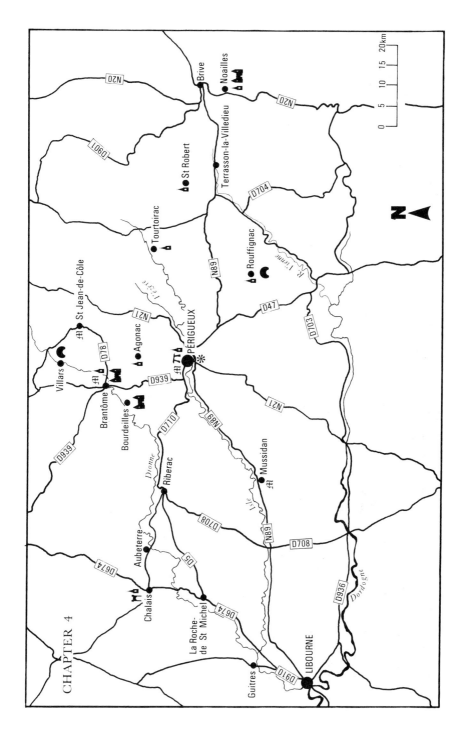

CHAPTER 4

Interior of St Front, Périgueux

St Front, Périgueux

what can only be described as a pâté farm. Here, in long cages, are kept the geese whose livers provide the basis for the great speciality of this region, *pâté de foie gras.* At the risk of putting the reader off the dish for life, the process may be briefly described. Briefly, the geese are force-fed until their livers become enlarged and degenerate, at which time they are killed. The liver, with the addition of slivers of truffle, becomes a highly prized delicacy, and commands a considerable price. At St Laurent, in a shop between the cages, tins and bottles of *foie gras* and other regional specialities are bought eagerly by passing travellers, seeming quite unperturbed by the scores of beady eyes watching them from behind the wire netting. The French, curiously enough, are not such great *foie gras* eaters as the English, probably because of the price. *Foie gras* tends to be a

PLACES TO VISIT FROM PÉRIGUEUX

Les Bories
Fine fifteenth-century castle on the Isle, open from July-September only.

Caudau Valley
Little-visited valley between Périgueux and Bergerac, above the Cingle de Trémolat.

Tourtoirac
Small quaint town north-east of Périgueux. The abbey there can be visited if you apply at the gate.

Rouffignac
Recently well restored after destruction in 1944. Sixteenth-century church. Also prehistoric cave paintings.

Chancelade
Abbey church dating from the twelfth century.

Mont Réal
Château fort on a hill overlooking the Crempse, south and west of Périgueux.

Agonac
A great market-place for truffles, and a fine fortified church dedicated to St Martin.

Sorges
A 'House of Truffles' at the Eco-Musée de Sorges, near Savignac-les-Eglises.
Open: daily except Tuesday, 2.30-6.30pm.
Tel: (53) 05 90 11

seasonal dish in France, eaten particularly at Christmas; hence perhaps the old rhyme which tells us:

> Christmas is coming, the goose is getting fat,
> Please put a penny in the old man's hat.

Turning off the road here, one reaches Athur, a small village which contains a Lanterne des Morts. These curious, hollow, pillarbox type structures are very rare, and no one seems to know when or why they were first erected. Certainly the one here is at least 300 years old, and probably much older. However, in spite of doubts about the origin, the locals are still putting the Lanterne to use. A watch-fire is lit at night whenever anyone of prominence dies, and from here, the highest spot in Athur, the Lanterne can be seen for miles around. It was last lit to mourn the death of General de Gaulle.

From Athur, the back roads lead down, across the River Isle, to Périgueux, and the view from the bridge over the river there gives the traveller a startling sight of the great cathedral of St Front. The saint himself was an apostle sent by St Peter to evangelise Périgord, where his tomb is mentioned as early as the seventh century, and was destroyed by the Huguenots in 1575. It lies by the pilgrim road from Vézelay to Compostela in Spain, and the cloisters contain Merovingian tombs.

St Front is one of those places, which although one has never seen it before, looks terribly familiar. One is reminded of the posters of the Blue Mosque in Constantinople. It even has a stunted form of minaret jutting out around the domed cupolas of the roof. As so often happens, however, distance lends enchantment, for nearby, the church is a disappointment. Inside, it is a vast, cold, stone cavern, dimly lit by the flickering candles of the faithful, and a place to escape from as quickly as possible.

Périgueux itself, however, is delightful. The old city which clusters close to the cathedral is a maze of narrow medieval streets and alleyways, which recall old times. Unlike some medieval cities, such as Carcassonne, Périgueux is big enough and prosperous enough not to rely entirely on tourism for a livelihood, with the result that many of its buildings are still lived in by families, or used as offices or workshops by small firms. This area would make a delightful artists' quarter; it has all the feel of one, and happily those buildings which felt their age and were crumbling are being carefully restored.

Périgueux is the capital city of the Dordogne *département,* as it was once the capital of Périgord. It has a population of some 50,000 and is the ideal centre for a holiday, or for exploring the region, situated as it is practically in the middle of the *département.* The tourist office near the cathedral is particularly helpful and should be visited, as should the Périgord Museum in the Cours Tourney.

The city is a gastronomic centre, an exporter of high quality foods, like pâté, and the home of several

Chancelade Abbey

restaurants which specialise in the local cuisine. Notable among these are the Restaurant Leon near the museum, and La Bousse. Périgueux suffered considerably in the Middle Ages and during the Wars of Religion, when Catholic and Huguenot captured the place in turn and did considerable damage in the process.

Away from the old quarter, around St Front, in what is now the more modern part of the town, on the road to Angoulême, are some even older sights, including the fine church of St Etienne de la Cité, which until 1669 used to be the old cathedral, although it was badly damaged by the Huguenots in 1577. Near St Etienne lies all that is left of the old Roman amphitheatre which could once seat over 20,000 people and is now a public garden. The amphitheatre's destruction began as early as the third century AD and now only the domed gateways to the old arena are left, through which one passes out to the street. It seems strange to walk along a passageway which once gave entrance to an anxious Christian or a hungry lion.

Périgueux, like the majority of French provincial capitals, was once a Roman town, *Vesunna Petrocorium,* and the site of a sacred spring. It remained a major city of Aquitaine until it was sacked by the Alemans in the third century, and was regularly pillaged in the centuries thereafter. Bertrand du Guesclin had his headquarters here and forayed out against the English in nearby Quercy, although the town was briefly ceded to the Plantagenets after the Treaty of Bretigny in 1361. It is a pleasant town and well worth a few days' stay, both to explore the town and as a centre for visits to the surrounding countryside.

From Périgueux an important detour to Brantôme should be made, and on the way to Chancelade, an interesting spot off the road just outside Périgueux. The abbey church there is functioning and services are still held there. This twelfth-century abbey is interesting to the present-day visitor because it retains many of the original monastic features. It comes alive to the visitor, and only the monks are missing. It has cloisters, a refectory

---

PLACES TO VISIT NEAR BRANTÔME

Château of Puyguilhem
Follow the D83 and 83 north-east from Brantôme, to the magnificent sixteenth-century Renaissance château of Puyguilhem, one of the most beautiful castles in Périgord.
Open: daily except Tuesday, 10am-12 noon and 2-5pm.

Grotto of Villars
On D82, north of Puyguilhem, deep grottoes complete with prehistoric cave paintings.
Open: 15 June to 15 September.

St Jean de Côle
A little-visited but very typical Périgord village, with a medieval bridge, ancient houses, and a Romanesque church.

Bourdeilles
Village with thirteenth-century castle on the River Dronne. Look for the water-mill under the old curved bridge.

and a guest wing, for monasteries were the hotels of medieval Europe, and most interesting of all, it has a well-watered carp pond. With Fridays and Sundays and innumerable feast days (which were really fast days) the medieval monks had a great appetite for fish. All abbeys had fish ponds and the huge, slow moving carp was a popular dish. Baked carp from the right cook was a dish fit for a king, and very gratifying for an abbot. The top of the tower at Chancelade can be seen from the Périgueux to Brantôme road, and this diversion is well

rocky outcrops on the hills, which were perhaps more easily seen when the region was less wooded.

Further along we come to the village of Château-l'Évêque. The château there is now a large and modern hotel, but seen from the road it is a most imposing sight, and while the hotel is very comfortable the atmosphere of a medieval fortress still remains. There are, however, large numbers of châteaux-forts in this area, so the one at l'Évêque need not detain us.

The attractions of the Dordogne are so many and varied, that in themselves they would justify the trip. The smaller villages, however, have one great advantage in that they provide the tourist with a reason for travelling across this region, where every turn brings fresh scenes and every view a new delight. It is good advice to forsake the main road wherever possible and strike out across country, heading in the general direction of the destination.

So, putting the theory into practice, one can strike off along any road more or less north-east from the Périgueux to Brantôme road above Château-l'Évêque and one will eventually come to Bourdeilles, which is a gem.

The setting, the castle above the river, and the tranquillity, all combine to make Bourdeilles an absolute must for any traveller. The position in the valley of the swift, shallow, sparkling Dronne is superb. The little town nestles, all white walls and red roofs, at the foot of a towering limestone yellow castle, round the walls of which the river

worth while.

This region is the Périgord Blanc, a wide strip of rolling, wooded, country which runs west to east, to the north of Périgueux, up to the frontier with Quercy. It is a limestone region, and it is said that the name comes from the white

The abbey at Brantôme

curves and bubbles. A mill beneath the castle walls parts the stream, which, in passing, turns the mill wheel, and sends the mill water rushing under the old curved bridge. Anyone would wax lyrical about Bourdeilles and still fail to describe it fully; it has to be seen.

The castle at Bourdeilles, which dates from the thirteenth century, was built by the French and surrendered to the English in 1295 by St Louis when he returned to them the French lands in Aquitaine lost by King John. Bertrand du Guesclin, France's Fabian general, recaptured it in the following century and it remained in French hands thereafter. The medieval

donjon, or tower, is open to the public, and a considerable climb is rewarded with views over the Dronne valley, while from the river one gets a view of the fine Renaissance building in the grounds. This was added to the castle in the sixteenth century and is the relic of a sad little tale.

Queen Catherine de Medici decided to take her son Charles on a tour of his kingdom, and the news caused a great stir throughout the land, with every landowner hoping for a royal visit. Jacquette de Montbron, the Lady of Bourdeilles, hired architects and masons and had this fine building erected to house queen and court, but they never came! The queen saw no reason to visit good Catholics who were already loyal, and passed by, to woo less staunch allies.

The writer, Pierre de Bourdeilles, was born in the castle in 1540. In his early life he was a soldier, and fought at Jarnac in 1569. He was a leading figure at the French court and a confidant of Henry II's wife, Mary, later Queen of Scots. After Jarnac, however, he returned to the abbey at Brantôme, and taking the town name as his *nom-de-plume,* began to write. His writings were anything but contemplative and his *Les Dames Galantes,* which gives a detailed, not to say intimate, portrait of various goings on at the court of the Valois, delighted his contemporaries and has been read with much scurrilous amusement ever since. Bourdeilles, or Brantôme as he is better known, died in 1614.

Brantôme is not far from Bourdeilles and is reached by a road flanked by the Dronne on one side and by limestone cliffs on the other. Down the centuries the river, hollowing out the valley, has carved deep holes in the limestone, undercutting the cliffs horizontally in places, until it is a wonder that they do not collapse. Near Brantôme the caves in the cliffs have either been turned into homes or incorporated into larger outside dwellings. Cliff homes are not peculiar to Dordogne and indeed one can see them along the Loire, but they are very common here and a feature worth looking out for.

Brantôme is a picturesque place with elegant buildings overlooking the Dronne and a fine abbey, where Pierre de Bourdeilles did his writing. The abbey was founded by Charlemagne and has been updated throughout the centuries. The little town is a delightful spot and contains two excellent restaurants, the Chabrol and the more expensive, but very good, Moulin du Roc. One for lunch and one for dinner would make a visit to Brantôme a gastronomic experience.

Further north lies the pleasant little town of Nontron, somewhat overshadowed by the charm of Brantôme and Bourdeilles, but well worth a visit, standing as it does on a beetling ravine, and a good centre for touring the northern marches of the Dordogne. Those who enjoy a good walk should go out on the road to Châlus and walk to the waterfall at Chalard, about half an hour from the road.

Heading south towards the Dordogne from Nontron, the road runs along a valley past Aubeterre and La Roche Chalais to the town of Coutras, which although outside our boundary is still within our story.

At Coutras in 1588, Henry of Navarre, later Henry IV of France, fought a decisive engagement against the army of the Catholic League, under their commander, the Duc de Joyeuse. Henry of Navarre was a strange mixture, a fine soldier, a great womaniser, fickle, irresponsible and dynamic. A typical Bourbon in fact. The Wars of Religion in France had settled into one long struggle between the Holy Catholic League, led by Henry, Duc de Guise, nominally acting for King Henry III of Valois, and the king's heir, the leader of the Huguenots, Henry of Navarre. This 'War of the Three Henris' as it was called, had been tearing France apart, but at Coutras the Catholic field army

PLACES TO VISIT FROM
TERRASSON-LA-VILLEDIEU

Noailles
South of Brive; has the splendid
Renaissance château of the
Noailles family, and the church of
St Pierre.

St Robert
On the D31, north of Terrasson,
the village of St Robert, where the
twelfth-century church has
magnificent ambulatory chapels.

under Joyeuse thought they had the
Huguenots in their net, and could
finish the war at one blow. They
could not have been more wrong.
Henry's cannon tore huge gaps in
the ranks of the League, and a single
cavalry charge broke the Catholic
army in pieces. In less than one hour
the battle was over and Henry was
master of the field. The Duc de
Joyeuse had been unwise enough to
order his men to take no prisoners.
Surrounded, he threw down his
sword, crying 'My ransom is a
hundred thousand crowns', but
nobody wanted his money and
someone shot him through the head.
This victory, however, which should
have put Henry in an unassailable
position, rewarded him not at all.
That night, leaving his army to head

back to its base in Béarn, he went
with a few followers to lay the
captured League standards at the
feet of his current mistress, La Belle
Corisande. Henry exemplified the
Bourbons, that family about whom
it was later said that they had
learned nothing and forgotten
nothing. That apart, Henry was an
excellent politician. He could make
statesmanlike remarks and gain
great credit for his integrity, and
then do precisely the opposite, and
still somehow justify it.

When it was pointed out that the
one great stumbling block to his
being declared the heir to Henry III
was his Protestant faith, he rejected
the idea of turning Catholic and
replied that a man's religion was not
to be taken off and put on like a
shirt. Protestant Europe thrilled, for
that was it, exactly! That said, and
the credit duly banked, Henry then
remarked that, after all, 'Paris is
worth a Mass', became a Catholic
and was duly crowned Henry IV. To
be fair, shortly after his coronation
he did pass the Edict of Nantes,
which granted religious toleration
throughout France.

From Coutras the road leads back
along the Isle Valley to Périgueux,
but at the western end of the
Dordogne *département,* the road
from Libourne back into it permits
an exploration of the marvellous
wine country of St Émilion.

5 Libourne to Bergerac

Libourne stands on the north bank of the Dordogne, at the point where it is joined by the Isle tributary, about twenty miles from Bordeaux by road and some fifty miles from the point where the Dordogne joins the Garonne to form the Gironde estuary. Directly across the river from Libourne the traveller enters wine-growing country on the peninsula which lies between the Dordogne and Garonne, and which is therefore called Entre-deux-mers. There is good wine over there, and a good tour across the vineyards to Sauveterre-de-Guyenne, but our road lies to the east.

Libourne itself was founded by an Englishman, Roger de Libourne, who was Seneschal of Gascony. It still has some of his medieval fortifications, notably the towers by the Grand Port. Libourne is a good shopping centre and an excellent base for exploring the St Émilion wine country to the east, or to foray across the river into Entre-deux-mers. The river is tidal here, with a

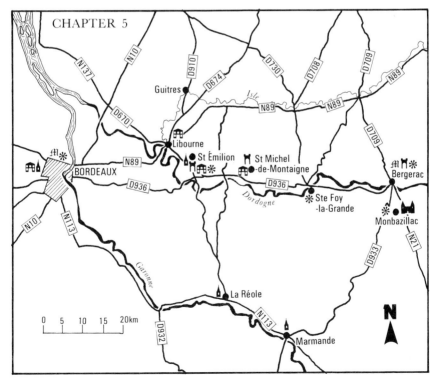

Libourne

PLACES TO VISIT NEAR LIBOURNE

Vaynes
On the south bank of the
Dordogne, below Libourne, a
river port dominated by a
château, once owned by Henry of
Navarre. See the dovecote.
Open: 1 July to 30 September,
10am-12.30pm and 2-6pm.

Grotto de-Pair-non-Pair
In the Moran valley near St
Antoine, this grotto contains
carvings of mammoths dating
from 30,000 BC.

Château de Breuilh
An eighteenth-century château
near St Antoine with a fine wine
cellar.

St Jean de Blaignac
Village on D670, on south bank
of the Dordogne, notable for a
fortified church.

rise of about ten feet, and the town
does duty as a small riverside port.

The main town in these parts is, of
course, Bordeaux, which has a
population of nearly half a million
and is a thriving industrial centre.
Bordeaux lies outside the scope of
this book, but as it owes its
development largely to the produce
of the Dordogne and the
Libournaise hinterland, it cannot be
entirely neglected, and a visit may be
entertaining.

Bordeaux is a very ancient city,
which flowered under the rule of the
Dukes of Aquitaine. When Eleanor
married Henry II, the export of wine
to England, which had already

begun, then flourished and has
continued to the present day. The
prosperity of Bordeaux was founded
on the wine drawn from the
vineyards of this area, and
incidentally, the then plentiful
English vineyards were suppressed
to provide the larger market for this
foreign import. Since the king's
main revenue was from his excise
duty, this is hardly surprising.

Libourne makes a good base for
this region and has an adequate
number of hotels at all prices,
mostly situated near the railway
station. The Hôtel Negrier is a good
place to stay.

Leaving Libourne the road goes
east for a few kilometres, and then
turns north for the wine centre of St
Émilion, a very fair town indeed.
There was a Gallic oppidum, or hill
fort, at St Émilion over two
thousand years ago, and there are
still traces of prehistoric, Gallic, and
Roman occupations. In the eighth
century, St Émilion, an anchorite
monk, had his cell here and founded
a small hermitage, around which the
beginnings of the present town
began to form.

St Émilion gained its charter from
King John, (or as the French call
him *Jean Sans-Terre,* John
Lackland), in 1199. At the same time
he appointed the *Jurade,* a body of
twenty-four men good and true, and
charged them with the task of not
only looking after the town and the
townspeople, but also maintaining
the standards and quality of the
local wine. Successive kings, French
and English, have confirmed these
rights and duties, and the *Jurade* still
rules to this day.

St Émilion is full of pleasing
attractions, not least the yellow,

Storing wine in the Médoc

WINES OF THE DORDOGNE

Travellers can take home a practical memento of their visit to the Dordogne with a selection of the local wine. The following are worth considering:

St Émilion:
La Tour du Pin, Château Figeac
Pomerol:
Petrus, Vieux-Château-Certain, Latour-a-Pomerol
Bergerac:
Reds
Monbazillac:
Sweet white
Montravel:
Whites. Try the Haut-Montravel
Cahors:
Reds. The 'Black Wine of Quercy'
Côtes de Duras:
Whites and reds
Gaillac:
A sparkling white. Try the Gaillac *Perle*

Wise travellers sample wines at *dégustation* stations, (wayside booths which can be found everywhere in the Dordogne) and buy a bottle or two of anything that takes their fancy, but bulk purchases, chosen from the list above, can be made inexpensively in any of the *hypermarche* (large supermarkets) in the area.

crumbling, honeysuckle-covered walls across the moat. Inside the walls lies a huge monolithic church hollowed out of the living rock, and crowned by a medieval steeple. The cloisters of the collegiate church, part of which is now occupied by the local *Syndicat d'Initiative* or Tourist Office, should be visited, for, apart from the fine medieval setting, it contains an enormous wine press and various other interesting implements connected with the cultivation of the grape. On the opposite hill lies the twelfth-century Château du Roi, which once was the only entrance through the walls; and it is from these walls, in a good year, that the vintage is proclaimed by the *Jurade*. Unchanged, the limestone rocks of St Émilion have been hollowed out to serve as wine cellars and here in the cool darkness, the rich clarets of the region can mature until they are ready to be sold, at ever-increasing prices to ever-eager buyers.

The word 'claret' comes from the French *clairet,* which means 'clear' or 'light', and the wines are so called because in the Middle Ages they

Wines in cask at Château Lafite

were found to be lighter both in colour and effect than the richer wines of Burgundy or the black wine from Cahors to the south. There are over five hundred square miles of claret vineyards to the east of Bordeaux, and they produce annually about a hundred million gallons of wine, which is still not enough to go round, so great is the demand for fine wines. Not all this wine is of the same quality, and those of St Émilion are fruitier and sweeter than those of the Médoc, which nevertheless means that they are very fine wines indeed to the average palate.

There are some ten square miles of vineyards in the area of St Émilion, and from the town itself there are vineyards in all directions, as far as the eye can see. Pomerol, Château Cheval-Blanc, Château Figeac and La Tour du Pin are

Caves at Montravel

Vineyards in the Medóc

expensive, but there are plenty of lesser-known wines at more moderate prices in the Côte de St Émilion. Examine the prices of the *Crus Bourgeois* for a possible bargain.

The town is a good centre for a walking tour into the local vineyards. Little paths wind everywhere among the vines, and the wine producers are happy to welcome visitors, both to sample the wine and buy a bottle to take away. It is noticeable that many of the vines have a rose bush or flowers planted at the end of each row. This certainly breaks up the otherwise monotonous green of the vines, but it is, of course, there to assist in the pollination of the grape. Even an industrious bee can get bored with vine pollen. Apart from the beneficial effect the rose has on the vine and the bee, the roses and the

vines make a fine walk on a warm summer evening. The vines flower in June, and the grapes are ready to be picked about three months later, when the fields are a maze of busy pickers, all hopeful that this will be not just a good year but a great year, and produce a claret to remember.

Needless to say, St Émilion manages to create some fine food to complement the local vintage. Try the *entrecôte aux échalotes* or the *poule-au-pot* at the Logis de la Cadene, or for the more wealthy, a full menu at the Hostellerie de Plaisance.

From St Émilion there are various roads down to the river, and to the east, but keeping off the main roads one can weave through the various vineyards and inspect their 'château' in passing. All Bordeaux wines, red or white, are 'Château' something, from the lordly Château Lafite, to the ordinary Château 'Plonk'. Some of the houses of the proprietors do indeed look like châteaux, but others just resemble large farmhouses, but a bottle of 'Farmhouse 54' would not be the same thing at all!

Down by the river bank, east of St Émilion, lies the town of Castillon-la-Bataille. The battle in question took place in April 1453, and was the final battle of the Hundred Years War, which drove the English out of Aquitaine and reduced their French possessions to the Calais *pale.*

The site of the battle lies outside the town on the plain to the left, just off the road to Ste Foy. A monument marks the spot there, an obelisk erected to the memory of the French soldiers and their two captains, Jean Burau, who commanded the artillery, and the Breton Count de Penthièvre, who commanded the *gens d'ordonnance,* and it is a worthy memorial to the early prowess of artillery, *ultima ratio regis,* the king's last argument. Castillon saw, at last, the eclipse of the English archer. For nearly a hundred and fifty years his harrow-shaped ranks standing quietly on a hillside, behind their hedge of stakes, had struck despair into his enemies, but the French knights would not play that game any more, and once his enemies refused to advance into the arrow storm, the archers' supremacy disappeared.

It is curious how the English soldier prefers to fight a defensive battle. From Senlac to Waterloo his greatest victories, often against great odds, were when he turned at bay and forced the enemy to attack him. Once firmly established, English infantry could not be easily

PLACES TO VISIT IN AND AROUND ST ÉMILION

Hillfort
Gaulish *Oppidium* dating from 2,000 years ago.

Monolithic Church
Hollowed out of the rock and crowned by a medieval steeple.

Château de Roi Castillon-la-Bataille
Site of the final battle of the Hundred Years War.

dislodged and the enemy could lose an army against their stubborn ranks. The French did have successes in battle during the Hundred Years War, although we do not read about them in the English history books. They were usually successful when they took the English army by surprise, or on the march, and could charge in before the archers could plant their stakes, but it took three generations for them to revise their tactics and force the English on to the offensive. When the French refused to advance, the English general, John Talbot, 'great marshal to Henry VI, of all his wars within the realm of the French', was forced to lead his archers to an assault on the entrenched French who had field artillery. The result was a disaster. In the battle fell the flower of the English infantry, the only field army they had was totally destroyed; worst of all, Talbot was killed, and he was irreplaceable. Talbot's son, young John, was killed in the first assault on the French position and when his father heard the news he turned back from the rout and sought his own death among his enemies, a wasted end for a man who, as Shakespeare put it, was 'England's glory, Gallia's wonder'. There is a monument to Talbot on the riverbank nearby, but it is little visited, and Castillon, a watershed in Anglo-French history, has disappeared into the list of long-forgotten battles.

The next stop on the road to the east is the little hamlet of Montcaret-Tête-Noir. This was a name to conjure with in the fourteenth century, for Geoffrey Tête-Noir, who lived hereabouts, was the most notorious and most successful captain of *routiers* in the French wars. From his base at Montcaret, he could, and did, demand ransom and tribute from travellers on their way to Bordeaux, whether they travelled by road or by river. Montcaret today has a fine old church, some Roman mosaics, and one small restaurant where a four-course dinner with house wine costs a very modest amount.

The small village of St Michel de Montaigne, north-west of Montcaret, lies on a hill dominated by an enormous château. The village is a small, quiet place, an unlikely home for the man whose reputation brings so many here, a reputation which has girdled the world and spanned four centuries.

Michel Eyquem de Montaigne was born in 1533, the son of a prosperous local knight, Pierre Eyquem, of Bordeaux and Montaigne. His mother was a Spanish Jewess, Antoinette de Lopez, and since the Jewish race descends through the mother, he was technically a Jew. It is an academic point, for Montaigne was baptised a Catholic, like his forefathers, and remained one all his life. He did, however, inherit from his mother the Jewish love of literature and the arts.

He was the eldest of eight children, and at sixteen went to the University of Toulouse to read law and philosophy. On coming down in 1554 he opened a legal practice in Périgueux, at the same time as his father became Mayor of Bordeaux, to which town Montaigne transferred his practice in 1557. This was during the early days of the Wars of Religion, and as they raged across the south, Catholic Bordeaux became the centre for the persecution of the Protestant Huguenots who, in turn, were harassing the vineyards in the surrounding countryside on which the trade of the port depended.

In 1565, Montaigne was married, wisely choosing a rich heiress, and when his father died three years later, Montaigne found himself a wealthy man, with land and property in both Bordeaux and Montaigne. He had six children, all but one of whom predeceased him, and he died at his home in Montaigne in 1592 at the age of fifty-nine. So much for his life, but what of his work?

During his lifetime he gained a great national reputation for his tolerance, rare at that time, his judgement, rare at any time, and his literary skill, but his great contribution to the world of letters was his invention of the 'essay'. The word 'essay' comes from the French *essai,* which means 'test' or 'trial'. In his essays Montaigne submits his

Tower of Montaigne

---

beliefs and ideas to tests of self-examination and his books of essays are a continuous test of his attitude to the world and its beliefs. He is nothing if not frank, and the essays reveal a critical style which is still entertaining today.

Montaigne was clearly a sceptic; 'Call no man happy until he is dead' was just one of his sayings. 'Although we sit in the highest throne in the world we still sit on our own tail' was another. He had his pen in his hand, his eye on society, and his tongue in his cheek, which is not a bad position from which to survey a reeling world.

With these many talents, Montaigne was much sought after as a counsellor. He became Mayor of Bordeaux and a confidant of Henry of Navarre. Indeed, Henry, laden with the standards of Coutras, stopped at Montaigne's home on his way to visit Corisande, and had Montaigne lived long after Henry was crowned, the king would have forced him to become the Chancellor of France.

Montaigne could have been anything he wished, but he was without ambition, and preferred to stay at home in his tower in the Dordogne and write. The only strong influence on his life was his close friend Etienne de la Boétie. The two men took to each other on first meeting, and their friendship lasted until la Boétie's death, a loss from which Montaigne never quite recovered. There are few signs of any other person or belief influencing Montaigne, but in an age torn by conflicting religious and political beliefs, he remained firmly on the side of moderation and tolerance.

It is this and his cheerful scepticism which makes him such a relief. Reading history one hears of people scourged and driven by passionate beliefs, often based on the most sketchy facts or reasoning. How refreshing to meet someone who not only viewed the whole world with total disregard, but also continued to do so when it was greatly to his material advantage to do otherwise! He was an adequate mayor of Bordeaux, but at that level he stopped. He retired at every opportunity to the tower in his castle at Montaigne and there he wrote away happily for as long as he lived.

His château at Montaigne was not the one we see there today. The original was destroyed by fire, although luckily Montaigne's tower survived and is incorporated into the present building. Here we can still see the rooms in which Montaigne lived and worked, with the beams covered with sayings from his favourite writers, Plutarch and Seneca. He could push back his chair and gaze up at these sayings, and no doubt would spend hours like that, or looking out from his tower across the valley and the

---

PLACES TO VISIT NEAR MONTAIGNE

Abbey of Blasimon
On D17, south of St Émilion, the Romanesque abbey of St Maurice.

La Réole
A pleasant village on D670, with ancient houses, remains of a medieval castle and a Benedictine abbey.

Marmande
A large village just inside the Agenais, east of La Réole. The church of Notre Dame is a beautiful example of the Gothic style; the cloisters are Renaissance.

Pessac
Church with Byzantine style belfry.

---

vineyards of the Dordogne.

He describes the tower in his writings, 'My tower has a chapel on the ground floor, and my bedroom on the second. On the third is my library, which is circular in shape, and being rounded it shows me all my books at once, arranged on five tiers of shelves. From this room I have open views, and sixteen clear paces to exercise. This is my throne and here I rule absolutely, reserving this one corner from all society.' He was a lucky man to have such a retreat and we, too, are lucky that so much remains to remind us of a man who, from a wealth of opportunity, had the wisdom to know the value of a little peace and quiet.

Monpazier, a bastide town

Wayside calvary at Tursac, near Les Eyzies

Les Eyzies from the hills near the cave of La Mouthe

Château Fayrac

Interior, Castle of Montaigne, showing some of Montaigne's favourite sayings

There is a main road on the north bank, but a side road goes down towards the Dordogne and across the river to the village of Pessac. The church at Pessac is worth seeing; it is the most jumbled structure, with a small Byzantine-style belfry graced by two large bells, which can be inspected before pressing on to Ste Foy la Grande.

Ste Foy lies on the south bank of the river at a point where two bridges cross it. One of the factors which makes travelling in the Dordogne enjoyable is that there are plenty of bridges, and one can cross from one side to the other with comparative ease. The nicest part of Ste Foy is the riverbank, which usually is crowded with fishermen. French fishermen never seem to catch anything, but they stand there for hours clutching their heavy poles (they are far too heavy to be called rods) and go home at last empty-handed. There are plenty of fish in the river and they jump in the evening up among the swifts and swallows darting after the low flies.

Ste Foy was held for the Protestants during the Wars of Religion, and was largely destroyed in the years of incessant warfare. Originally it was a *bastide*, built as a fortified town in the fourteenth century, but the fighting of the sixteenth century has destroyed much of that graceful medieval feeling, and only the straightness of the streets and the connecting alleyways, typical of a *bastide*, give a clue to its first foundation. There are more *bastides* in the country to the south.

There is a short, but worthwhile, detour to the Château de Duras, where they have a good dry white wine at a very reasonable price, and a few bottles of this wine will be a useful memento.

Ste Foy possesses two pleasant hotels, the Boule d'Or, and the Cheval Blanc, both of which have reasonable prices and accommodation, and adequate restaurants. It is, therefore, a pleasant place to stop and prepare for further exploration up the river.

6 The Bastide Country_

The journey upstream to Bergerac reveals a change in the Dordogne valley. Above Bergerac the hills edge down from the north, and near Lalinde they reach across the river past Couze and carry on rising until they topple over into the valley of the Dordogne's sister river, the Lot, further south across the *bastide* country.

Bergerac itself is the largest town in the central Dordogne, and as a focus of road and rail traffic is a well developed commercial centre. In spite of this it exercises a considerable charm, and has an enterprising history drawn more from fiction than reality, but none-the-less entertaining.

Bergerac is famous as the birthplace of Rostand's tragic hero, that peerless swordsman and silent lover, the man with the fatal nose, Cyrano de Bergerac. Cyrano is not just a theatrical character; he actually existed. In Rostand's creation he was the archetypal Gascon, one of those gallant

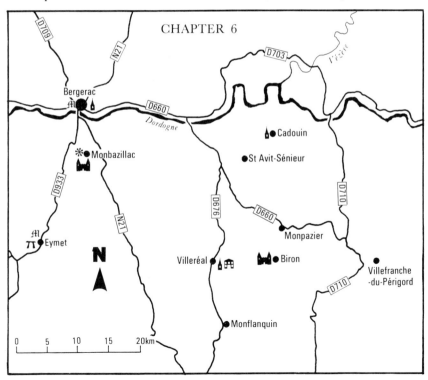

CHAPTER 6

67

Fortified church, Bergerac

soldiers, 'whose only fortune was a sword and a few barren acres to starve on', who flocked into the armies of the Sun King, and carved out a place for themselves in French history. D'Artagnan, who also actually existed and was indeed a captain of the King's Musketeers, is yet another Gascon and one whose colourful career is well-known to Englishmen through the fictional pages of Alexandre Dumas. The people of the Dordogne are Gascons. Putting aside precise geographical considerations, they are Gascons in the same way that many Londoners born far from the sound of Bow Bells claim to be Cockneys. The Dordogne area was, for much of its history, in Gascony, or Guienne, or Guyenne or Aquitaine, a variety of names which

Vineyards at Monbazillac

all add up to much the same thing.

Bergerac, like Ste Foy, was a Huguenot town, and was largely destroyed in the Wars of Religion; one exception was the old church of Notre Dame in the Place Gambetta, which survived this period. After the Revocation of the Edict of Nantes in 1685, when Louis XIV stripped the Protestants of their rights to religious toleration, most of the Huguenot population fled abroad and the town went into decline. It was saved from total extinction by the introduction of tobacco, which grows well in the local countryside.

Bergerac is the major centre of France for the growing and processing of tobacco and has a Museum of Tobacco which traces

Monbazillac Castle

PLACES TO VISIT IN AND AROUND
BERGERAC

Château of Monbazillac
South of Bergerac among the
vineyards, this castle dates from
1550.

Moulin de Malfourat
The windmill has lost its sails,
but the site commands fine views
as far as Biron.

Biron Castle
A beautiful village and a fine
castle.

Museum of Tobacco
Shows development of the
tobacco industry from the
sixteenth century.

growing of that other staple
commodity, the fine red wines of
Bergerac. One can sample them, and
much good food, at Le Cyrano's in
the Boulevard Montaigne.

Across the river, heading towards
the *bastide* country, the road runs
through more vineyards, but these
produce the local white wine,
Monbazillac. This is very sweet, but
it is the wine of the Dordogne, and if
one simply asks for a glass of wine
hereabouts, Monbazillac is offered.

The village of Monbazillac has the
usual imposing château, built about
1550. There are wonderful views
from its grounds back over the
Dordogne valley towards Bergerac,
and for a more sweeping panorama
the traveller can visit the Moulin de
Malfourat, only a few kilometres
away, as the main road leads to
Eymet, where there is a *bastide*.

The word *bastide* comes from the
French *bâtir*, to build. From about
the middle of the thirteenth century,
the English and French kings sought
to consolidate their holdings in the
south-west by constructing a series

the development of the trade from
the sixteenth century. It is also a fine
shopping centre, and the principal
market town for the local
agriculture, which includes the

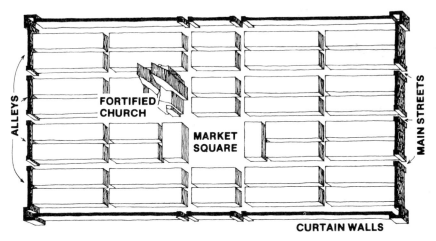

Diagram of a Bastide town

of fortified towns. They discovered that simply to stud a land with castles and garrison them with soldiers was not enough. If a land was to survive as anything other than a desert, it must be supplied by an industrious civil population, who could not maintain themselves on the march without protection from those mercenary scourges of the Middle Ages, the *routiers.* By the fourteenth century the *routiers* had become organised, and in their so-called Free Companies lived entirely off the land and its inhabitants. They called themselves the *Tard-Venus,* the Late-Comers, and in peace or war they made the land a living hell. Some Free Companies were very large. When the English captain, John Hawkwood, took his White Company to Italy, it is recorded that he had over 200 mounted men-at-arms and 1,000 English archers, so it is little wonder that his arrival in Italy proved so decisive in the wars between the city states.

From about 1250, *bastides* began to appear, as small fortified towns. In them the inhabitants enjoyed many freedoms, from taxation for example, and as a bonus were frequently granted holdings outside the walls, while the town was usually given a charter for a weekday market. Whether French or English, they were usually built on the same lines; a rectangle with high curtain walls, each street running at right-angles to the next, and with narrow alleys or *canyiou* linking each main street. In the centre was a covered market hall, and the church was usually fortified as a last refuge should the outer defences be overwhelmed. A typical *bastide*

PLACES TO VISIT IN THE BASTIDE COUNTRY

The bastides of:

Villefranche-du-Périgord
Villeréal
Monpazier
Monflanquin
Eymet
Beaumont

The castle of:
Bonaguil
Fifteenth-century fortress, in very good condition.
Open: Easter to 30 September.

Sauveterre-la-Lemance
Ancient fortress once belonging to the Kings of England. To visit, apply to the guardian.

looked like that in the diagram on page 71.

The rectangular blocks of houses could each be defended in turn, while the alleys could be used for outflanking movements or retreats, and were too narrow to enable a mounted knight to use his weapons. Another typical feature of the *bastide,* and one which, happily, remains in use to this day, were the *cornières,* or arches, which formed the lower storey of the houses in the central square. Under these arches the merchants could have their shops and display their wares, and they are still used for the same purpose today, with the shopkeeper living over the store.

Bastides were built all over the south-west, and throughout Old

Languedoc, but the most attractive are in the south of the *département* of Dordogne, in the hilly country overlooking the Lot.

Eymet, south of Bergerac, was a French *bastide,* and is still in an excellent condition, with the arcades decorating the main square, and a medieval castle, now somewhat in ruins, just by the church. Near this château is the municipal *'camping'.* There are many campsites in the Dordogne, and while some are better than others, all are very good. The one at Eymet is typical and is worth describing as a guide to the rest. Situated on a large, tree-lined lawn, it has a resident manager, showers, lavatories, sinks for washing clothes, swings, and a sand-pit for smaller children. It is, at the most, two minutes from the centre of town and cost only a few francs per day for full use of the facilities. With everything in such excellent order, camping does seem very good value, not that the hotels in the town are expensive, and the traveller usually gets excellent value for money there.

East of Eymet lies the picturesque little town of Issigeac. Issigeac is not a *bastide,* but is such a lovely little place that no tour of the Southern Dordogne should omit it. The road to Issigeac is a delightful run, and so beautiful is the countryside that simply to stay in the car is

73

Château de Castlenau

impossible. A walk across the meadowland is a sheer delight in the early summer, for apart from the host of blue, red and yellow flowers, clouds of butterflies of all colours start up from the grass and flutter about knee high.

The country has, however, every

appearance of a frontier march. A number of hills are crowned with watchtowers and the farms cluster tightly on their hilltops, the older ones bearing every sign of defensive construction. This country east of Issigeac forms part of the Périgord Noir, lying south and east of Périgueux, and straddling the river west of the Vézère valley.

From Issigeac the road south out of the Dordogne leads to another French *bastide,* Villeréal. The road to Villeréal offers some wonderful views, and more signs of fortification. Villeréal stands on the little River Dropt, a pleasant stream, and it is a pleasant little town, built in 1265 by Alphonse de Poitiers, the brother of St Louis, in an attempt to prevent further advances to the north by the English. Make a note of Alphonse de Poitiers, for he was a town planner of distinction. Villeréal fell to the English during the Hundred Years War and remained in their hands for many years.

The church and covered market were also built by Alphonse de Poitiers, the walls of the church being immensely thick and sturdy enough to withstand the cannon of the Huguenots when they attacked the town in 1572, although the outer façade of the church suffered considerably. Seen in the sunlight, with vines trailing down the walls of the golden stone houses and hovering over the geraniums, Villeréal is a lovely spot, but it lies not in the Dordogne but in the *département* of Lot-et-Garonne. However, it is a town worth seeing.

A bicycle would be an excellent way to travel around the *bastide* country for these little towns are easily within a couple of days' ride from each other, and the quiet passage of a bicycle seems very suited to this mellow landscape.

A turning on the right off the road from Villeréal to Monpazier takes the traveller to the mighty château of Biron — what a place! Many castles in the Dordogne are big, some — Hautefort for example — are large, but Biron is vast. Castles were not built as pretty toys, or to give credence to the newly-won nobility, but for war and defence in time of war, to nail down an uncertain frontier in the interests of the lord, and their tall, thick, crenellated walls give ample proof that in their day, before the coming of artillery, and even afterwards, they were formidable fortresses.

Biron, the village as well as the castle, is a dream. The church which stands below the walls of the castle is a beautiful building, with a Renaissance house built into one side, and the whole is so well matched and finely formed that one could sit and gaze at it for hours. The castle stands on a mound which is itself on the top of a small hill. It was built over many centuries, but the bulk of the construction dates from the sixteenth century, and the most attractive feature is the entrance. The visitor climbs up a steep ramp, so little used that grass grows quite thickly in the verges. At the top one is confronted by a massive door, the sort that would seem more natural to beat with the butt of a lance. Beside the door hangs a chain which, when pulled, clangs a large bell suspended overhead. The head of the *châtelaine* appears over the battlements; having seen who it is, she descends to open

The Dordogne Valley

---

the door with much dragging of bolts and rattling of chains — just as most travellers have entered the castle in the past, and so much nicer than a turnstile and a ticket desk. Inside, the castle is wonderful. The views from the walls are breathtaking, and the castle has everything a medieval castle should have; a dungeon, ramps and battlements, a huge kitchen and a wonderful chapel with the effigies of some of the previous owners.

In the sixteenth century Biron was the home of Charles de Gontaut, soldier and intimate (like his father before him) of Henry of Navarre. When Henry came to the French throne as Henry IV, he richly rewarded his old comrade-in-arms, whom he created admiral and later a Marshal of France, awarding him the barony of Biron and the governorship of Bordeaux. But de Gontaut was one of the people who felt that even half Henry's kingdom

Cadouin Abbey

would not be enough, since he had helped the king gain all of it. He plotted to betray the king and divide his kingdom. When his plot was discovered, Henry forgave de Gontaut and returned his possessions, only to be betrayed again by another plot. Henry offered to pardon de Gontaut yet again if he would just kneel and ask forgiveness, but the proud servant refused. Having no option, the king

Cloisters, Cadouin

ordered his execution and de Gontaut was beheaded outside the Bastille in 1602. Curiously enough, his father also lost his head, struck off in battle by a cannon-ball.

Biron is a wonderful castle, and a must for any visitor to the Dordogne, though it does not, in fact, receive many visitors. In an average year, only some 5,000 people visit it, yet the castle is large enough to absorb that many in a single day.

The next halt is the beautiful *bastide* of Monpazier, perhaps the most attractive of all the southern *bastides.* Monpazier was an early *bastide,* founded by the order of the English king, Edward I, in 1267. His seneschal in these parts was Pierre de Gontaut, an ancestor of Marshal Biron, who oversaw the construction of the town, which changed hands several times during the Hundred Years War. Monpazier has all the finest features of a *bastide,* a fine covered market, a

fortified church, much reconstructed in the mid-sixteenth century, and the usual alleyways and arcades. Monpazier today is in some danger of becoming chic. Some of the arcades have become sites of fashionable little shops, but the town has enough charm to beat off the forces of commercialism.

Villefranche-du-Périgord, the next *bastide,* lies south-east of Monpazier and is yet another beautiful little town in the typical *bastide* fashion, with a most splendid covered market, a fine church, and, more recently, an excellent hotel and restaurant, the Commerce, overlooking the valley of the Lemance.

Villefranche, as the name implies, is a French *bastide,* built once again by Alphonse de Poitiers around 1270. It is a pleasant town and something of a leisure centre, with riding, tennis, swimming and cycling all catered for and energetically enjoyed by crowds of youngsters.

PLACES TO VISIT NEAR
VILLEFRANCHE-DU-PÉRIGORD

Monpazier
Bastide town with market,
church, hotel and restuarants.

Siorac
Village with campsite and a Logis
de France.

Cadouin
Cistercian monastery and home
of the 'Holy Shroud'.

Bannes
Château on the River Couze.

The road north, to further
bastides and the Dordogne, takes
one to the little village of Siorac
which, apart from an excellent
camping site on the very banks of
the river, contains the wonderful
little Auberge de la Petite Reine, a
Logis de France, which is always a
good sign. Here there is a fine
dining-room and, very welcome in
the heat of the day, a swimming
pool. The *petite reine* is the wife of
the owner.

At Siorac one can turn west to
visit the Cistercian monastery at
Cadouin, where the story of the
Holy Shroud is an object lesson in
the advisability of leaving well
alone. The possession of relics was
one of the passions of ecclesiastical
foundations in the Middle Ages, and
some time after the First Crusade, in
the early years of the twelfth
century, the monastery of Cadouin
acquired the piece of linen that had
reputedly been wrapped around the
head of Christ after the Crucifixion.

Possession of such a relic brought
fame and great wealth to the
monastery; pilgrims, rich and poor,
humble and mighty, came from all
Christendom to visit the Shrine of
the Shroud. This useful traffic
continued until the early years of the
nineteenth century, when a monk
with more learning than brains
decided to have the shroud
examined by experts, and they not
only dated it about AD 1100, but
stated that the embroidery on the
hem was Arabic! Within months the
dreadful news was out, and the
pilgrimages to Cadouin promptly
stopped. Today Cadouin is a quiet
place with no crowds waiting
patiently before the great doors of
the Romanesque abbey, but one
imagines that when the curious
monk came up for his next
penitential scourging, his brother
monks laid on the strokes with a
particular will!

Near Cadouin lies the English
bastide of Beaumont, built at the end
of the thirteenth century and still
retaining, apart from the usual
bastide features, most of the original
fortifications. Here is a riot of
flowers, in particular pots of dark
red geraniums which are set off so
beautifully by the grey-gold of the
sunlit walls. Beaumont has two lines
of walls, the outer carrying the
narrow ring road at its foot, and the
inner offering a wide grassy footpath
for a circular tour of the town. It has
a fine church inhabited in summer
by squadrons of swooping swifts,
swallows and martins, which nest in
the high corners of the huge
building.

The road from Beaumont back to
the Dordogne takes one beside the
little River Couze, a noted trout

stream, and past the towers and pinnacles of the castle of Bannes. Bannes is a fairytale castle, the type in which the golden-haired princess always lives, and, set as it is on green wooded hills, it seems to epitomise the legends of chivalry and romance, which a visit to the beautiful *bastide* country vividly recalls.

Across the Dordogne at Couze the road east comes to Lalinde, also a *bastide* but one which, after some industrialisation, bears little sign of it. Lalinde does, however, contain the fine and reasonable Hotel du Château, which stands right on the banks of the sparkling Dordogne and appears at first glance to be constructed mainly of ivy. Dinner on the terrace there makes a perfect ending to the day.

7 Prehistory in the Vézère Valley

The study of prehistory is a comparatively new branch of archaeology. The word 'prehistory' was only coined in 1851, and to understand the subject the word needs some definition. Essentially it records the history of man in those ages before history was, or could be, written down. In the purest sense, all Man's past, from yesterday to the dawn of time, is history, whether recorded on papyrus or stone, or simply deduced from the artefacts and waste which history has left behind. Prehistory needed a finer definition than this because,

certainly in the seventeenth and eighteenth centuries, any idea of Man's history being unwritten would have been regarded as heretical, or patently absurd, for all men knew that Man's history had been carefully recorded from the moment of creation in the pages of the Old Testament.

Dr John Lightfoot, Vice-Chancellor of Cambridge University, in 1642 made the following statement: 'Man was created by the Trinity on 23 October 4004 BC at nine o'clock in the morning,' and this statement was

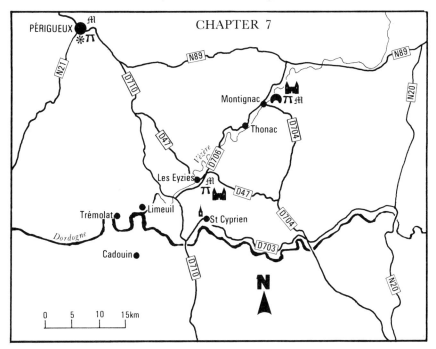

OTHER ATTRACTIONS NEAR LES
EYZIES

St Cyprien
Pleasant village on the
Dordogne, with vast
Romanesque churches.

Couze-et-St Front
Little village on the Dordogne,
with a fine Romanesque church.

Cadouin
Site of an abbey founded in 1115,
once containing the 'Holy
Shroud'.

not really challenged for the next hundred and fifty years, in spite of the expansion of Man's knowledge. It was, after all, quite possible to fit the Persian, Greek and Roman empires into a past of nearly six thousand years. Even Stonehenge, or Carnac in Brittany, or the finds of the early archaeologists which did not seem to fit any known epoch, failed to distort the tacit acceptance of Man's divine origin. It was the geologists who brought prehistory into the light. In their study of the earth's strata (a study very fashionable in the eighteenth century), a continuous stream of curious objects was discovered, some animal-like fossils or the bones of strange beasts, other items like stone axes and flint arrowheads, clearly with human connections. It then became accepted that Man had an early ancestor who lived in caves and hunted his prey with stone weapons. Then, in 1816, a Dane, Christian Thomsen, first defined the three historical Ages of Man, and named them the Stone, Bronze and Iron Ages.

The Three-Age System, as it is called, although very simple and obvious to us now, made a great impact at the time, and has indeed endured as the basis for all age-stratification in archaeology. It soon became apparent that the Stone Age had lasted a lot longer than the other two, and the Stone Age itself came to be subdivided into the Old Stone Age or Palaeolithic, the Middle or Mesolithic, and the New or Neolithic. It also became clear that of these three subdivisions, the Palaeolithic had been by far the longest, and in turn it needed subdividing.

Modern Man does not need to be told that the pace of life is getting quicker; although expressed in thousands, and tens of thousands of years, that is what has been happening since Man first appeared on the earth's crust, about a million years ago. Each age, and sub-age, has been shorter than the previous one. The earliest Man, so far discovered, lived about 100,000-40,000 years ago, and from the discovery of his remains at Neanderthal, near Dusseldorf, we call him Neanderthal Man. He lived in the Middle Palaeolithic period, was a cave dweller, and used stone and flint weapons. Neanderthal Man stayed around for a long time, gradually evolving, and one of the places where he had left many traces of his development is along the valley of the River Vézère in the Dordogne. Neanderthal Man developed what is known as the Mousterian culture, based on hunting and cave dwelling.

The Dordogne area was below the

The Dordogne near Limeuil

limit of the advancing ice in the last Ice Age, and in the caves and hollows of the limestone cliffs early man could build shelters and survive. As a result of these settlements, the Dordogne has made a significant contribution to the study of prehistory, and following the practice of naming discoveries after the place in which they are found, the region has contributed Mousterian, Cro-Magnon and

Symbolic Statue of early man at Les Eyzies Museum

Magdalenian Man to our knowledge of the human species and his development down the millennia.

About sixty thousand years ago a more developed group of Neanderthal people were living in the Dordogne. They are called Mousterians after a cave at the village of Le Moustier five miles north-east of Les Eyzies. A partially excavated rock shelter can be seen in the village, and a narrow path beside

PREHISTORIC SITES TO VISIT IN
THE DORDOGNE

Les Eyzies

The centre for prehistory in the area and a visit here is a necessity. See Museum of Prehistory, the Cro-Magnon shelter and various caves in and around the village.

Padirac

This cave was once considered the gateway to Hell, and it served as a shelter for the local inhabitants in times of strife. No paintings but a fascinating trip.

Pech Merle

This cave contains carvings and paintings of the prehistoric era. It was discovered in 1922 and is said to rival Lascaux. The visit takes one hour through $2\frac{1}{2}$ miles (4km) of caverns.

Font de Gaume

Near Les Eyzies. Many cave paintings of the Magdalenian period.

Presque

Near Padirac, south of Montal. This cave is full of stalactites and curious rock formations but no paintings.

Cougnac

Near Gourdon. Two large caverns. The *Salle des Peintures Préhistoriques* has black and ochre paintings of elephants and ibex.

Rouffignac

The caves are 3 miles (5km) south of the village and contain Magdalenian paintings and carvings of ibex, rhinos and mammoths.

Lascaux

Cave paintings from 17,000 years ago (closed to public).

Lascaux II

Splendid replica of original painted cave exhibiting paintings of 17,000 years ago.

it, leads up to the cliff above where a fine dwelling site is preserved. It should be realised that men lived in overhanging rock shelters like this, and not of course in the deep, dark underground caves. Cro-Magnon man who appeared about 40,000 years ago is the first true *homo sapiens* recognised, and is named after some burials excavated at Les Eyzies, in what is now the garage of the Cro-Magnon Hotel. Even more developed men, whose work is called Magdalenian, are named after a rock shelter where they lived beside the river Vézère at La Madeleine near Tussac found in 1863. It was Magdalenian Man who executed the world famous wall paintings at Lascaux, about thirty thousand years ago; (all these dates are very general, and, as dating techniques are revised, become changeable, but as steps in Man's development, they are still valid).

The whole area of the Vézère valley is one great prehistoric site. Rock shelters, painted caves and working places abound, and archaeologists and spelaeologists are

Museum of Prehistory, Les Eyzies

Rock carving, Les Eyzies

still delving ever deeper into the hills of the region, probing under the crust to see what fresh evidence can be discovered.

The Vézère joins the Dordogne at Limeuil, and the road follows the winding course of the Vézère, on one bank or another, all the way up to Montignac. Prehistoric sites lie on either side of the road, which is flanked by steep limestone cliffs which contain holes and caves obviously not of natural origin. Past Le Bugue one reaches the town of Les Eyzies de Tayac, which was for a time the home of Cro-Magnon Man.

Cro-Magnon Man was discovered here in 1865 by some workmen digging a road. They found a rock shelter containing the skeletons of a whole family, two adults and three children, who were eventually classified as from the Upper Palaeolithic era and called Cro-Magnon. The Cro-Magnon Hotel now stands on the site of the discovery.

Above the hotel, built into an old prehistoric rock shelter and the remains of a medieval castle, is the National Museum of Prehistory, at which any tour of the valley ought to start. This provides the visitor with full information, although only in French, on the development of Man. Outside the museum stands a huge statue, symbolizing all our early ancestors in one huge, bewildered, shambling brute, who bears little resemblance to any of them. The actual Cro-Magnon, whose skull inside the museum indicates, was of modern appearance, and quite a good looking creature.

There are two exceptional caves at Les Eyzies, beside the road to Sarlat. The first is Font de Gaume with

---

PLACES OF INTEREST IN THE VÉZÈRE VALLEY

Roque St Christophe Le Moustier
Cave dwellings in the cliffs on five levels.

Grotto of Le Grand Roc
Large cavern hollowed out of the limestone by water action.

Museum of Spelaeology
Exhibition of caving techniques and discoveries.

Gorge d'Enfer
Various rock shelters.

---

painted bison and engraved mammoths. Sadly the pictures are fading badly, and the cave is so popular that long queues form early in the morning throughout the summer, and it is often necessary to buy your ticket for the following day.

Slightly further east along the road is Les Combarelles, a long narrow cave containing hundreds of engravings, which is almost as popular as Font de Gaume.

Visitors taking the road from Les Eyzies north-east to Montignac will come to Le Thot, a centre for the interpretation of prehistoric art. Using multi-screen slides and films, tableaux, and a park containing examples of the animals shown in prehistoric paintings, visitors get an excellent introduction to prehistoric art. Details of opening times can be obtained from the market square in Montignac.

Before reaching Le Thot visitors may like to divert to the south-east on the outskirts of Le Moustier to the Roque-St Christophe, a great rock face half a mile long which rises above the Vézère valley. Cut into this are various terraces on some of which prehistoric man lived, although it was greatly altered during the Hundred Years' War. It is evidence of this later period that one see today.

This cliff fortress, for that is what it is, is on five levels, reaching a total height of almost 300ft (90m). The cliff drops sheer away to the Vézère, and the tour should not be attempted by anyone who suffers from vertigo. Here are the caves where medieval man lived, the recesses for water, the niches for fires, the places on the cliffs where animals were tethered, and the painfully hacked out staircases which gave access from one level to another. This trogolodyte village must have been impregnable to anything but starvation.

The Roque was occupied by bandits who ravaged the surrounding countryside until the Lord of Limeuil captured the place in 1400, and hanged everyone who survived his assault. The Roque is quite alarming enough to climb in peace time, and anyone wishing to make a thorough exploration should have a good head for heights.

Les Eyzies is not really attractive. It is organised to cope with the visitor, and although a pleasant town with plenty of good hotels (often booked-up months ahead), camping sites and restaurants, it gives one no feel for what the valley, or life in it must have been like for prehistoric man; although after six o'clock when the tourists have left, peace and quiet descends on the town and one can stroll by the river, or along the footpath directly under the cliffs. One does have the modern compensation of a meal at Le Centenaire; the *escalope au saumon* is not cheap, but excellent. British visitors may draw the line at the local delicacy *caille:* quails, tiny birds whose heads look up pleadingly at you from your plate.

A curious natural sight at Les Eyzies is the Rocque de la Peine, a cliff eroded by wind and rain which hangs out over the road on the southern outskirts of the town.

On the western side of Les Eyzies, and signposted for miles around, lies the Grotto of Le Grand Roc. This is a large cavern without paintings, hollowed out of the limestone by the action of the water over countless centuries. Wonderful stalagmites and stalactites rise and fall everywhere, and the whole cavern is well lit, to bring out the colours of the crystallised limestone. This cave was located in 1924, and is visited by thousands of poeple every year, though it is quite claustrophobic. The Grotto is reached by a low narrow tunnel 130ft (40m) along, with thousands of tons of rock above.

Just past Le Grand Roc is a prehistoric site of the Magdalenian period at Laugerie Haute, where excavations have been left open for visitors, but where the guide only speaks French. Along the same road is the Museum of Spelaeology describing the geology and pot-holing activities of the area. Outside, one can visit the Gorge d'Enfer which has various rock shelters, one of which contains the most wonderful carving of a huge fish nearly four feet (1.2m) long. The

Montignac, on the Dordogne

gorge also harbours much wildlife, with nightingales nesting on the high cliffs, and the birdsong in the early evening is quite deafening.

Although the prime attraction of the valley of the Vézère is the prehistoric sites, it has had a long history in more recent times and contains some attractive villages and castles, notably the fortified church at Tayac.

Above Le Bugue lies the pleasant village of Campagne, which has a fine castle built in the fifteenth century, and situated in a small park just beside the road.

It is curious that the existence of prehistoric man could so long have been ignored when successive generations, down to quite recent times, used the same caves and shelters and must have passed on the knowledge of their existence from father to son by word of mouth over the centuries. The inhabitants of the Vézère valley must, over the centuries, have noticed something unusual, or at least different in their valley, and the area is not remote. Nevertheless, it is only during the last hundred years that any major prehistoric discoveries have been made.

The cave at La Mouthe, which has some fine engravings and a few paintings was the first to be discovered in 1894. Visiting it today retains much of the atmosphere of the original discovery, since it is not lit by electricity and one is accompanied by the local farmer or his wife with an acetylene lamp. Bara Bahau near Bugue at the lower end of the valley, was not investigated until 1951. The tiny cave of Comarque was not discovered until 1915; it is actually under the castle there and not open to the public.

As one can see, this area is full of prehistory and the interested visitor is advised to stay at Les Eyzies or Montignac and explore the region thoroughly. Prehistorians and pot-holers flock to the Vézère from all over the world, and their researches are now creeping back up the Dordogne valley towards the still unexplored areas of the Massif Central.

Nevertheless, in spite of a century of exploration the most famous discovery in the region has become a modern myth sadly distorted by time and only partly true. Even so the real story is worth telling.

The cave had been known since the 1920s as *le trou du diable,* when its entrance was revealed by a falling tree. No one bothered to explore it, until on 12 September 1940 five schoolboys were looking for a secret gang headquarters and chose the cave, which today is called Lascaux. They were astonished to find great paintings on the walls; cows and bulls jostled with red deer and prancing horses. The boys were fascinated and gazed entranced until the batteries of their torches gave out and they made their way back to the surface.

Cave paintings were no real novelty to the children of Montignac and it was only in the course of conversation that the boys mentioned the find to their schoolmaster, who made them take him to the cave and relocate the entrance. With a proper light they had a good look at these astounding sights. This was 1940, and wartime, but the news quickly reached the noted French archaeologist, Abbé Breuil, and broke upon the world.

Lascaux is remarkable. The history of archaeology records no other place like it. The paintings are superb works of genuine primitive art. The colours are fine and clear, still vivid after twenty thousand years and date from the Upper Palaeolithic period, having great precision and purity of line. Particularly striking are the colours. The great red cattle and the yellow deer are remarkably vivid, and the film of crystal which has seeped from the walls has preserved the colours with remarkable clarity. Or rather it had until 1940. Although it was wartime, people flocked to Lascaux in massive numbers, and although every care was taken, more damage was done to the paintings in the next twenty years than in the previous twenty thousand. The heat generated by the crowds and the movement of air caused a rapid deterioration in the paintings, and, regrettably, the cave was closed to the general public in 1963. Today, only a few visitors are admitted, usually those with special archaeological connections, or reasons for visiting the caves. It is always worth applying, and, to those with good reason, permission is usually granted. Meanwhile there are excellent reproductions on view at the site of the cave, perched on a tree-clad slope, and a trip to the area is a pleasant excursion. It is a pity that such great art must be kept from public view, and perhaps one day a method of preserving the paintings will be found, thus enabling the cave to be opened once more. However, there is no need to feel disappointed, because there are many other prehistoric caves in the area, some of which have paintings. Well worth a visit are the caves already mentioned at Les Eyzies, Pech-Merle, Cougnac, Rouffignac, all with wall paintings, and others at Padirac and Presque which have spectacular stalactite formations.

In 1983 the Department of the Dordogne opened Lascaux II, an extremely accurate reproduction of half of the original Lascaux cave near Montignac. Constructed with the help of computers and stereoscopic photographs, the painter Monique Peytral has reproduced with great accuracy two galleries, the Hall of the Bulls and the Painted Gallery. The reconstruction is buried in a disused quarry about 200m from the original cave, and is now entered through a museum gallery which gives the history of the original cave which can be dated to 17,000 years ago. Tickets for Lascaux II can be bought in the market square of Montignac and visitors should note that it is very crowded in summer with long waits for entry.

From Lascaux the traveller can choose a number of ways back to the Dordogne, to continue the journey upstream.

One good route lies through Rouffignac, west of Montignac, which has a fine sixteenth-century church, the only building to escape destruction when the Germans burned the village as a reprisal in 1944. Now largely rebuilt, Rouffignac is a pleasant spot set among rolling hills. The village contains the largest of all the prehistoric caves in the area and huge crowds visit it in the summer to take the electric railway deep into the hillside to see the hundreds of engravings and paintings. Mystery surrounds this cave and many British archaeologists consider that a number of the pictures are modern additions, although the bulk are genuine. From Rouffignac it is only a short run to Vergt, the site of a great battle in the Wars of Religion, and now famous for strawberries. From there the road south runs past the castles at Gaubertie and Montastruc, and back to Bergerac.

8 The Castle Country

The next two chapters describe the course of the River Dordogne from Bergerac to Beaulieu. It changes greatly in this section, as does the country through which it passes, and this change becomes noticeable as one moves east and north, climbing towards the Massif Central and the source of the river.

During this journey we pass through castle country; for a time it seems as if every rock and hilltop, every cliff and crag is crowned with a fortress, and this is almost true. The middle of the Dordogne is thronged with castles and they give to this naturally beautiful countryside a great air of gaiety, chivalry and romance.

This, historically speaking, is quite correct, for the very idea of

romance was introduced to the western world by the lords and ladies of the Languedoc. They cannot have conceived the mischief they were making. Up to the twelfth century, the idea that a man and woman should or ought to love each other as a basis for a happy life together was not merely unthought, but unthinkable. Marriages among those of gentle origin were frequently contracted at birth by the parents, as a basis for the merging of property or to cement an alliance. No woman was expected to love her husband, and the husband was not expected to be faithful to his wife, for what had to be given as a duty could hardly be regarded as a gift. In Languedoc all this was changing, and the fashion of wooing a lady,

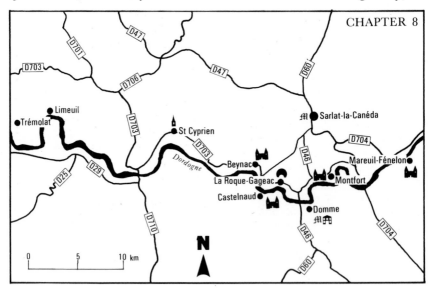

CHAPTER 8

competing for her favours and falling blindly in love, was accepted as one of life's more delightful attractions, but one reserved, be it noted, for married ladies only.

The unmarried ones were carefully chaperoned and while they would consider their social life a disaster without a string of gallants serenading them at their windows, or wearing their colours in the joust, it usually went no further than that.

It is very unlikely that any knightly swain received much physical reward for years of adoration of his chosen lady, but the very idea that a lady of reputation could have an admirer, who broadcast his love and passion for her around the castle, would have given any baron from north of the Loire cause to saddle his warhorse and look out his heaviest mace, while down south it was all part of the excessively enjoyable pastime of courtly love.

Needless to say, that gay and enchanting lady, Eleanor of Aquitaine, was a prime mover in this field, and at her father's court at Poitiers she held Courts of Love, at which her ladies and their followers discussed the finer points of romance and judged each other's skills in the affairs of the heart. It was all very harmless, and although Eleanor reputedly had affairs, notably when she accompanied her first husband, Louis of France, on the fiasco of the Second Crusade, there is no real proof that she ever went to bed with anyone other than her husband.

Aquitaine, with the bright sunlight, the beautiful countryside, and the clear air, is the place for romance, a land well fitted for lovers, and in the castles of

PLACES TO STAY AT OR DINE IN WHILE VISITING THE CASTLE COUNTRY

The two main towns hereabouts are Limeuil and Sarlat. Accommodation can be difficult to find in July and August, and it is as well to book ahead for a bed or a table in a restaurant. Apart from places mentioned in the text, the following are excellent:

Hotel Scholly
Hotel and restaurant at Siorac-en-Périgord.
Tel: (53) 28 60 02

Hotel Bonnet
Logis de France on the river at St Cyprien.
Tel: (53) 29 50 01

Hotel l'Esplanade
Logis de France in Domme.
Tel: (53) 28 31 41

Royal Vézère
An excellent hotel, full of information on the area, at Le Bugue.
Tel: (53) 06 20 01

La Hoirie
Pleasant hotel, $1\frac{1}{4}$ miles (2km) north of Sarlat. Try here before going into the town or ring and book ahead.
Tel: (53) 59 05 62

Hostellerie de Meysset
A country hotel above Sarlat.
Tel: (53) 59 08 29

Dordogne, a lot of loving, mostly unrequited, did fill the major part of the medieval day.

From Bergerac the road runs due east, along the north bank of the river through Lalinde, and on towards Trémolat. By the castle of Badefols, at the hamlet of Sauve-Boeuf, one can turn right on to the north bank of the river and proceed almost at water level as far as Mauzac. The Dordogne at this point appears to be a wide, shallow river, with wide gravel banks in midstream, and reeds and rushes floating close to the surface of the water. This is, in fact, something of an illusion for the height of the stream, here and elsewhere, is controlled by a series of dams and barrages where the water is diverted to produce hydro-electricity. One such barrage, with huge iron sluices, spans the river at Mauzac. Behind

the barrage the river rises by about 20ft and becomes instantly a slow, grave stream. Below the barrage, notices along the banks warn the public of dangers of camping on the islands mid-stream, or wading out to fish. The operation of the sluices can make a rapid difference to the level of the water and cause the unsuspecting angler or camper quite an unpleasant surprise, but the compensation lies in the vast views of the river obtained from the heights above the Cingle de Trémolat.

These *cingles,* or bends, are caused by the harder levels in the limestone forcing the river away from its natural course until it forms a great loop. The effect from the viewpoint by the Hotel Panorama is wonderful. The cliff drops down to the river far below, while on either side the river sweeps round the

The Dordogne at Limeuil

At Limeuil, where the Vézère joins the Dordogne, stands the beautiful Pont Coude, which spans both rivers at this point. Le Pont Coude means 'the elbow bridge', and that is exactly what it is, but how much better it sounds in French! Limeuil is an attractive town with curtain walls and a lot of medieval homes. The Dordogne is shallow again here, which gives some indication of how rapidly the land is rising, flowing fast again over gravel banks. The southern road from Lalinde reaches the far side of le Pont Coude and this route may appeal to those who do not want to face the climb up over the *cingle,* and it also gives excellent views of the limestone cliffs that contain the river in this section. It is best to cross the river here and continue on the southern bank.

The first castle which looms up past Siorac is at Berbiguières, a seventeenth-century pile which is challenged from the north bank by the sixteenth-century château of Fages on the green slope on the far hill above St Cyprien. This southern road gives wonderful views into the valley and over the river, and by veering down towards the river one comes on a block of castles, all different, and all picturesque. It should be remembered that in France a *château* can be any large country house, while a battlemented castle of the medieval period is more correctly called a *château-fort.*

To the fine château at Les Milandes the celebrated exotic dancer, Miss Josephine Baker, once the toast of Paris, retired, with her

opposite point, two great arms enclosing a green hill. Across the water, bridges march at intervals, stepping down the river like rungs in a ladder. The *cingle* at Trémolat is particularly beautiful, and the views over it from the north bank bring people from miles to admire the landscape below.

Trémolat itself, below the hill which overlooks the *cingle,* is a pleasant village, with a fine fortified church (and a massive place it is), without charm and with all the marks of a stronghold. Trémolat, thanks to the deepening of the river caused by the barrage lower down, has become a great centre for water sports with rowing, canoeing, sailing and water-skiing all taking place in the summer months. It is also a great cycling centre. Cycles can be hired in the village and the roads round about are full of cycle-parties.

CASTLES TO VISIT IN THE
DORDOGNE

Fages
Now being restored.
Open: Easter to mid-September.

Les Milandes
Originally built in 1489, much
restored and very beautiful.

Veyrignac
Seventeenth-century château,
burnt in last war, now restored.

La Treyne
A magnificent castle dating from
the fourteenth century.

Belcastel
Castle in private hands, but
gardens can be visited. Apply at
the gate.

Beynac
The most spectacular castle in the
area, high on the cliffs.

Castelnau
This castle overlooks the
Dordogne, near the junction with
the smaller Céré.

large family of adopted children. Set among deep woods, amid beautiful gardens, it is a wonderful place for children, and would that more people could put their retirement to such good use. The children have grown up and gone away, and Miss Baker is no longer alive, but she did a lot of good here and it is worth remembering.

Not far from Les Milandes, just by the road, lies the lovely château of Fayrac, which is practically a château-fort. Fayrac was the home of Henry of Navarre's great captain, Geoffrey de Vivans, stormer of cities, and it glowers across the valley to the town and castle of Beynac on the far shore. Beynac is a splendid place, as befits a town that was, in its time, the centre of one of the four great baronies of Périgord. Beynac, too, was a Huguenot stronghold, and together with Fayrac they sealed off the valley from the Catholic West. To get to Beynac you drive along to the bridge at Castelnaud Fayrac, where the fine castle of Castelnaud stands 1,000 feet above the valley on a great green hill. The castle was built in the twelfth century and changed hands several times in the Hundred Years War. The views over the valley from Castelnaud are fantastic, and the castle has recently been well restored.

Beynac was occupied and held in fee, that is, at the king's pleasure, by Mercadier, who was the captain of Richard Coeur-de-Lion's *routiers*. The castle was largely rebuilt in the thirteenth century and was one of the places where the *parlement* of Périgord met in the Middle Ages. The town of Beynac itself is full of fine medieval buildings and the climb up to the castle is, to say the least, invigorating, but a meal at the beautiful Hôtel Bonnet back down by the river would repay anyone for the effort.

Beynac castle is a splendid pile, full of good architecture; it is sad that the medieval lavatory — a hole in a window seat sealed with a stone bung — attracts the most attention!

Along the road from Beynac lies the riverside fortress of La Roque

Beynac on the Dordogne river

Domme

Fayrac

Gageac. Here, on the site of a medieval fortress similar in style and intention to the cliff dwellings of Tayac, a modern terrace of houses has been built in the style of medieval dwellings. If proof were needed of the attractions of pure style fashioned in natural materials, this is it. The houses rise and fall with the cliffs in a series of terraces connected with wide steps, and blend with the cliffs in a manner most pleasing to the eye. The site itself is an unlikely one, braced up hard under the cliffs, with only the road to separate it from the river. The river here is very popular with sunbathers, swimmers and fishermen, for the gravel banks make perfect suntraps and many people seem to manage both to bathe and fish, wading into the river waist-deep to cast their lines. The river is put to good recreational use and the camping sites along the banks are really wonderful. All are placed at attractive spots and even in the high season do not seem overcrowded.

La Roque Gageac has one of the passenger ferries across the river which supplement the numerous bridges. This one is operated by a cable and can take passengers across the river quickly.

At La Roque Gageac the route turns north, to Sarlat, the main town serving this part of the valley, and the home of Michel de Montaigne's

The Dordogne Valley and the Château de Fayrac

Beynac

great friend, Etienne de la Boétie. Montaigne was twenty-five when he met la Boétie, and they instantly formed a friendship which endured until la Boétie's early death. Montaigne refers constantly in his essays to la Boétie, and la Boétie was clearly one of great, if not the only, human influence in his life. 'If you ask me why I love him,' he writes, 'I can only say, because it was he, because it was I.' La Boétie died in 1563 and Montaigne was desolate.

La Boétie was born in 1530 in a fine house of the mid-fifteenth century, just opposite the cathedral, and has more claims to justify his memory than his friendship with Montaigne. As the Magistrate of

Sarlat he upheld the law in an unbiased fashion and, although a devout Catholic, extended the protection of the law to Huguenots. He translated various works from the Greek and made significant contributions to the common understanding of contemporary French political thought.

Sarlat, now the centre of the Sarladaise, once the capital of Périgord Noir, is a tourist centre and a market town, with a large colony of artists, some of whom display their wares outside the church of St Sacerdos, as merchants and craftsmen must have done for a thousand years. The church, named after one of those obscure saints

Sarlat; Hôtel de Glezêl

Vineyards near Sarlat

after whom the French usually chose to name their cathedrals and great churches, was rebuilt in 1504, and is undergoing significant reconstruction. In the churchyard is another of the peculiar Lanterne des Morts, much larger than the one at Athur near Périgueux, and local legend has it that this one was erected at the wish of St Bernard of Clairvaux, who preached the First Crusade from this spot. Lanternes des Morts are curious. No one seems to know why they were built, and no one feels certain enough to advance a positive theory. The one at Sarlat is certainly big enough to contain coffins, and one theory is that they were built to hold the bodies of plague victims or lepers, or strangers who died in or around the town and whose bodies had nowhere to rest while they awaited burial in consecrated ground. The light in the lantern would keep people away from the area of infection.

Sarlat gives one the feel of a medieval town. Like Périgueux, it has always been prosperous and large enough to live on its own wealth and industry and not need the present wealth of tourism. The visitor to Sarlat will get more feel of the Middle Ages during a quiet walk in the cathedral than from watching a full-scale medieval joust laid on by the local riding club and *Syndicat d'Initiative*. Sarlat is an attractive place and I suggest you go there for a stay, possibly at the Saint Albert hotel.

Leaving Sarlat and heading south towards the river again brings one to the little village of Vitrac. There are some splendid walks along the valley, and some fine fishing, and 1½ miles (5km) south of Vitrac, across the Dordogne, lies the fortress of Domme. Domme is an enchanting little town, beautiful at first sight, and even more beautiful when being visited and explored. Anyone would wax lyrical about it and for perfect beauty it is beyond description. Domme stands, a jewel in golden stone, on a tall hill overlooking a switchback, winding, road which heaves itself up through a just-wide-enough gateway into the outer square of the town. Domme is a *bastide*. The beauty of these foundations is so outstanding, especially when one remembers that they were built for war, that we can only

Walls of Domme

wonder at the skill of the architect in creating something so fine. The town was built for Philippe le Hardi, King of France, and has all the usual *bastide* features, though without the arcades. The town rises and falls over the hilltop, with straight streets and alleys linking up the fortifications. In one of the towers, that of the Porte des Tours, the visitor can see the names and arms of the captive Knights Templar, many of whom were incarcerated here after the Order was suppressed by Philippe le Bel in the fourteenth century. The present inhabitants of Domme are clearly as impressed with the beauty of the place as is the summer visitor, for they enhance the charm of the town with pots and baskets of flowers, long window-boxes, and neat gardens to provide bright splashes of colour against the golden stones.

From the heights of Domme, views over the river valley are naturally wonderful, and lunch on the terrace of the hotel there must be one of the most satisfying meals in the world, even without the excellence of the menu. Mighty Domme, once the key to the southern *bastide,* is still conquering people who come within her walls, by her outstanding beauty.

When Domme was built, she was declared by Philippe le Hardi to be impregnable; but it was his words rather than his actions which gave him the nickname of 'the Bold'. In fact Domme, like most other towns, changed hands regularly in the Hundred Years War, and was re-fortified and supplied with cannons by the Catholics when the Wars of Religion swept over this part of France.

Domme indeed justified the faith of her creator for many years, in fact until the year 1588, which proved so decisive for Protestant affairs in Europe, with the English defeat of Spain's Great Armada. The Huguenot cause in the south-west had also been going well since Coutras, and Henry of Navarre's great captain, Geoffrey de Vivans, who had already taken Sarlat,

moved his army against Domme. De Vivans had been born nearby at Fayrac, and therefore knew Domme well, including the reputation it had for being impregnable. He was aware of the strength of the great curtain *bastide* walls and, one would like to think, he hesitated before smashing such a beautiful town with his siege artillery, so he decided therefore on a stratagem. At night, with a party of only thirty unarmed men, he scaled the walls above the cliffs, rightly suspecting that the heights would be deemed unscaleable and lightly guarded. Meanwhile, his army made a noisy demonstration before the gates, and under cover of the noise and

---

Market hall and Church, Domme

confusion, de Vivans and his party entered the town and overcame the watch. Before the garrison knew what was happening the main gate was in their hands, and Huguenot cavalry were racing through the streets of the town.

De Vivans held the town for four years until 1592, and established it as the centre of Protestant power in the middle Dordogne. When he finally left, having sold the town to the Catholics of Bordeaux, he marched out with all the honours of war, standards flying, drums beating, and matches lit, leaving behind a town undamaged in the wars and very largely as we see it today.

Before leaving Domme, the traveller should walk along the ramparts, go down and visit the grotto in the limestone cliffs, and visit the little chapel of Cenac, not omitting to admire the views across the valley to Montfort and Beynac.

9 Eastern Dordogne

After Domme, as it passes through more of the castle country between Montfort and Beaulieu, the river changes. It is now a very steady stream compressed by the encroaching foothills of the Massif Central or, more precisely, above Souillac, by the Causse de Martel, one of the plateaux that reach down from the central mountain range. During this chapter the river leaves Périgord at Souillac and enters Quercy, turning north towards its birthplace in the Massif Central. The river remains charming and the countryside is full of interesting sights. The scenery changes only in that it adds grandeur to spectacle. High, forested cliffs encage the river, a foretaste of the mountains to come, and the sweep of the hills is magnificent.

The most wonderful thing about this Dordogne country, apart from the weather and the remarkable absence of crowds, is the continual supply of beautiful sights, both man-made and natural. Every day the

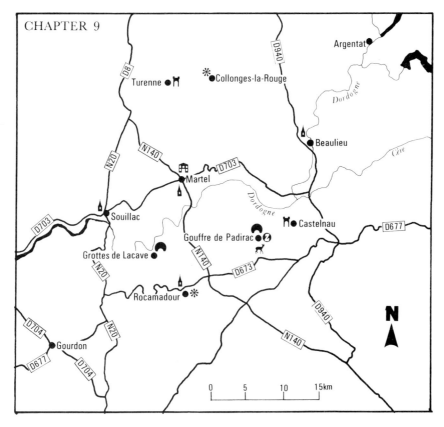

Mule team in one of the woods in the Dordogne

traveller sees something which seems unsurpassed so far, and then discovers either that same day or the next, something else, not better perhaps but just as beautiful, and very different.

Variety is the ingredient that prevents even beauty itself becoming monotonous. Louis XV's doctor once remarked, admittedly in a different context, that variety is the greatest aphrodisiac. He was, of course, a cynic, but the variety of Dordogne is certainly the reason why the traveller falls in love with the region — Hautefort, Brantôme, Bordeilles, the *bastides,* Biron, and latterly Domme — all are wonderful, yet none is in any way like the others.

From Domme, perched high on a hill on the south bank, one crosses the river to Vitrac, where there are some fine hotels, up to the great castle of Montfort. This is the classic castle of the Dordogne, the one which appears in all the posters, and on approaching it, one can see why. It is a large and beautiful place, so secure and solid on the very verge of the sheer drop down to the river that one imagines it being built inland, on safer ground, and then slid sideways into place.

Montfort perches on the cliff like an eagle, and from such an eyrie a watchman can scan the river valley for miles as it passes below in the sweep of the Montfort cingle, and like the Cingle de Trémolat, this sweeps north, with the castle at the apex of the curve, and the river falls away on either side below the walls.

The castle has had a long and warlike history. It was built in the twelfth century, and in 1214 was stormed and taken by Simon de Montfort, not the victor of Lewes and founder of the English Parliament who died at Evesham, but his grandfather, another Simon, who later led the Pope's army south in a Crusade against the heretics of Albi. He took the castle and held it for his own, and began the first of many alterations and reconstructions.

On such a commanding site, it was the scene of much fighting during the Hundred Years War, and was captured by both French and English in their turn. During the Wars of Religion, it fell to the Huguenots. Every siege destroyed some part of the fabric, and every rebuilding added to the castle's beauty and variety. The castle today contains a mixture of every period from the twelfth to the sixteenth centuries, but is largely fifteenth century and still inhabited, part of the keep containing an excellent restaurant. The view from the walls is naturally superb and the castle attracts crowds of visitors in the summer months.

Near Montfort lies the pretty village of Carsac. There was an abbey here in the Middle Ages which is now the village church. This has undergone the most careful reconstruction since the war, and the old medieval framework is now shown to good advantage. The churchyard is a riot of wildlife, with vivid green lizards scampering over the stones, butterflies hovering among the grasses, and the usual clouds of swifts and swallows darting about the sky.

In an area as devoted to agriculture and field sports as the Dordogne, there is naturally an abundance of wildlife. Most noticeable to the casual traveller are the clouds of butterflies which flutter everywhere in the deep meadows and along the grassy banks beside the roads. One frequently hears economists lamenting the inefficiency of the French farmer and the low level of productivity on the farms. If this is partly due to traditional methods of cultivation and the restricted use of chemical sprays, then the world at large has much to be grateful for, since these sprays have destroyed the British butterflies which were once so common; even now to see any at

Wine tasting

all is a rare event on a country walk. In the Dordogne the lepidopterist would be in paradise, while the traveller can again enjoy the pleasures of just sitting on a wall and watching beautiful butterflies flit aimlessly about. Birds, some familiar and others more exotic, are common, and the woods and fields are full of birdsong. Deer frequent the high Causse country and the smaller mammals, such as fox, weasel, squirrel, and rabbit are frequent sights, sprinting across the road. Domestic animals abound, sheep and cattle in the meadows, horses for work and recreation, while every farm has bright brown hens pecking happily around the yard, and a scurry of rabbits from hutches along the wall of the barn.

The great domestic bird of the Dordogne area is, of course, the goose. Doomed to be fed to death, they march in large companies around the fields with a gaggle of goslings hard behind, elbowing each other out of the way in the effort to keep up with mother. They seem surprisingly unferocious. Goats, too, are a common sight in the area, where their milk makes the delicious *fromage de chèvre*.

Food is an important part of a holiday, and in a land like the Dordogne, with so much to offer, a constant temptation. This can only be coupled with the fact that in French eyes, the cuisine of Périgord is one of the marvels of France. Dishes cooked *à la Périgordienne* are cooked in walnut oil, from the many walnut trees, and flavoured or garnished with truffles, the so-called 'black gold of Périgord'.

Truffles, as we have mentioned, live off young oaks, and can only be obtained fresh in November or

Château de Fénelon

December. The summer visitor is, therefore, not likely to meet a truffle face to face, in a state of nature as it were, which may well prove a blessing in disguise. The truffle is a wonderful catalyst for enhancing the flavour of an omelette or pâté, but on its own the truffle has the appearance and consistency of coke. It makes up for its indifferent appearance by a most pungent and penetrating aroma, which is not so much unpleasant as unavoidable. Truffles are not pleasant to keep around, but as an ingredient to im-

prove the flavour of some other dish they are delightful. A museum of truffles has opened recently in Sorges (see Chapter 4).

Omelettes made from the fresh eggs of farmyard fowls are always good value, while the local *omelette aux cèpes,* made with a variety of wild mushrooms, is a feast which with a good local pâté or *terrine,* and taken with a glass of Bergerac or Cahors, makes a perfect lunch.

Other specialities of the region include duck, guinea fowl and, of course, the goose, prepared in various ways and usually garnished with truffles. Fish, especially trout and salmon, appear on most menus and are well prepared. The great joy of the area, for the northern visitor, is the fruit. Peaches, cherries, apples, and pears grow here in profusion, and, freshly picked and juicy, make a perfect end to the meal. Strawberries are another local delicacy, and Vergt, in the Dordogne, is the strawberry capital of France. The strawberries are usually marinated for a few hours before serving in a dish of claret and sugar. This brings out the flavour of the fruit most effectively.

The local liqueurs also come from local produce. Two regularly offered as digestifs are the *eau de vie de prunes,* and the *eau de noix,* this last a speciality of Martel in the Causse. The former can be sampled in *dégustation* centres, and once tried will be found not at all unpalatable.

It will be seen, therefore, that the cuisine of Périgord is one of great variety, and any gourmet who makes the journey there will have no cause to lament the trip. Meals from the smaller restaurants' menus can be thoroughly recommended for they provide fine dishes at low prices.

Crossing the river east of Montfort, and turning towards Veyrignac, brings one to the fine castle at Fénelon, which offers the visitor spectacular views over the river, north towards Rouffillac. Fénelon has great curtain walls, dating from the fifteenth century, and some fine towers, but is chiefly noted as the birthplace of the writer François de Salignac, who was born here in 1651 and in later life, at Carennac, wrote extensively under the name of Fénelon.

Over the river again, blessing the abundance of bridges, we go through Rouffillac and along the north bank towards Souillac. The Causse de Martel comes sweeping down to the river here, and a quiet, bare wall of white limestone overlooks the valley as we come into Souillac from the west. The river here is again wide and shallow, dotted with the odd small island and with plenty of fine *'campings'* in evidence along the banks. Above Argentat the river is controlled by high dams,,but below it makes a perfect path for canoeists, for shallow draft canoes alone can cope with the low stream and the fast water.

By entering Souillac we have moved out of Périgord and into the eastern province of Quercy, the land of dovecotes. Souillac is a fine town, the largest in this region of the Dordogne, and dominated by yet another of those domed and minareted churches of the Périgordien-Romanesque type which we first met at Périgueux. The cupolas look quite out of place around the other medieval buildings of the French south-west, giving a Byzantine air to the church. This is probably where the style came from, for many men from the town and district went on the First Crusade, and undoubtedly returned impressed with the buildings of Constantinople, then, and for three hundred years afterwards, the greatest city in the known world. The great church of Souillac is worth inspection. Perhaps the men of Souillac erected it to remind them of the time when they were young, and fighting the Infidel in Outremer.

Interior of the château de Fénelon

Whatever the reason, this church and those others like it, are remarkable sights. This at Souillac was, like many of these large south-western churches, once an abbey, and is now the church of Ste Marie. The tympanum over the west door relates the cautionary tale of Brother Théophile, who badly wanted to build the church, when the Devil, who feels very much at home in these old Angevin lands, heard his prayer and offered to lend him a hand at the usual price of his soul. Luckily when the time came for the monk to pay up, the Virgin intervened and saved poor Théophile from his most unpleasant fate. These carvings are well worth seeing, for they are extremely clear, and rather disturbing. Overlooking the square stands the clocktower of the church of St Eloi, which is a landmark when seen from the surrounding hills and overlooks the entire town.

The English burnt the town during the Hundred Years War, and in 1562 it suffered the fate of Domme and Sarlat, and fell to the Huguenots, who made it a centre for the Protestant religion. Nowadays it makes a good centre for exploring the middle river or the Causses, and the Hôtel la Renaissance or the Hôtel Périgord are both very comfortable, with good menus available containing local dishes.

Following the course of the increasingly winding river, the next visit is to the picturesque seventeenth-century castle at La Treyne, which, seen from the bridge over the river flowing swiftly below

113

Fontaine de St Georges
A beautiful green spring where
the Causse Gramat meets the
Dordogne valley, off N140 above
Mont Valent.

Valley of the Alzou
The River Alzou runs south-east
from Rocamadour through
picturesque gorges. A good
walking route leads south from
Rocamadour.

Moulin de Saut
A waterfall at the ruin of just one
of the watermills which once
dotted the Alzou river.

Fénelon
Fifteenth-century curtain wall
with fine towers. Birthplace of
the writer François de Salignac.

the walls, is a fine sight. Here the
river contains submerged tree trunks
and great branches, relics of the
winter rains. West of La Treyne
where the Dordogne is joined by a
tributary river, the Ouisse, the aptly
named Belcastel stands on a cliff
over the river. This really is the
'beautiful castle'; not even Montfort
is as well situated, with the blue river
winding below the sheer white cliff
and the green valley and hills
cupping the castle on every side.
Belcastel was largely reconstructed
in the last century and from the
terraces below the towers wonderful
views can be obtained over the
valley far into the distance.

To the east of Belcastel in a region
of subterranean caves and grottoes,
lies one of the great natural wonders
of France, the great cave and underground river at Padirac. This is one
of the sights that the visitor to the
region must not miss, and if, as is by
no means impossible by now, the
appetite for castles and churches has
been filled, then a visit to Padirac
will be a refreshing change. It has
long been a popular spot for visitors,
and over the years a considerable
tourist complex has grown up
around the grotto. There is, for
example, a zoo, a bird park, several
restaurants, and some nice bars. In
the sunshine it all looks very
pleasant and relaxed, and those who
do not relish a trip to the bowels of
the earth will find plenty to entertain
them until the family returns from
below.

The great hole of Padirac was
once thought to be a gateway to
Hell, and it was not until 1889 that
the underground river, below the
hole, was discovered. Over the next
ten years expeditions pushed deeper
and deeper into the caves and, in
1947, by introducing a coloured dye
into the water, it was confirmed that
the waters eventually flow into the
Dordogne near Montvalent over five
miles away. The cavern itself, which
is huge, was created by the action of
rivers under the Causse de Gramat,
until they eventually forced a way
through the soft sub-strata to the
main river. The action of the water
has created great stalagmites and
stalactites, and a number of
underground waterfalls which
prevent the river being navigable for
the entire length. To visit the cavern
the traveller descends some three
hundred feet, by a series of lifts.

Padirac is very large, without the
oppressive closeness of the Grand

Padirac caves

Roc at Les Eyzies and no one who feels fine on the London Underground will be distressed at Padirac. It would be as well, though, to take an anorak or raincoat, for, be it ever so hot above, down below it strikes chill, with a steady rain of drips falling from the cavern roof far above. Once below, one proceeds along well-lit passages to the embarkation point for a cruise along the river. The trip is taken in flat-bottomed punts poled by guides in the manner of Venetian gondoliers, who keep up a continual patter of information.

The water is crystal clear, and, where it is too deep, the poling is off the walls, for the river passage, though often high, is never very wide. After almost a mile you alight at a small jetty where the guides take you on a tour of the waterfalls and the great cavern, which you ascend in a series of steps before returning to your boat again. The total trip takes about an hour and is a definite experience, not to be missed.

Back on the surface we follow the Dordogne again, north to visit the beautiful abbey at Carennac. The village of Carennac has some fine medieval houses, and is the centre for the production of the potent *eau de prunes,* but is historically famous for its connections with the writer François de Salignac, or Fénelon.

Within the abbey walls of Carennac, Fénelon wrote some of the great classic works of the French language, notably his *Télémaque.* Fénelon was prior of the abbey and the little island in the Dordogne opposite the walls is popularly supposed to be the 'Ile de Calypso' featured in his work. In all events, it is pointed out as such to the visitor, and one should not doubt a good story. Carennac was a Cluniac foundation, and dates from 1050, but when the abbey was suppressed in 1788 only four monks still lived there.

Along the river now, to Bretenoux, where the Dordogne is joined by yet another of her many tributary rivers, the Cère, running in from the east. The Dordogne changes direction here, heading north past the great red walls of the castle at Castelnau. Castelnau is a fine *château-fort* and very old, with parts dating back to the ninth century. In its hey-day during the Middle Ages, it was a major garrison, housing many archers and men-at-arms. North on the west bank, one finally reaches the historic and beautiful little town of Beaulieu.

Standing at the meeting point of three former provinces, Périgord, Quercy, and Limousin, Beaulieu is an old town, where the Benedictine

PLACES TO VISIT FROM SOUILLAC

Collonges-la-Rouge
North-east of Souillac, across the Causse de Martel, and a splendid drive.

La Treyne
A late-medieval castle to the east of Souillac on the banks of the Dordogne, much restored in the seventeenth century.

Gourdon
South of Souillac, just in the *département* of Lot, and capital of the green *Bouraine* country. See the fortified gateway.

Cahors
An hour's run south of Souillac, and a centre for the black wine of Quercy. Not to be missed if you are this close is the Pont Valentré.

Cales
Try to visit this remote little village near La Treyne, for the setting alone is worth the trip.

abbey, like the castle at Castelnau, dates back to the ninth century. The west door is intricately carved with scenes from the Day of Judgement, and the whole building is very striking. Nearby, overlooking the river is the Penitents' Chapel, another fine building, although, like the church, currently in need of some restoration. Beaulieu itself, the 'beautiful place' is the last river town we shall visit. From here the road runs up to Argentat, above which the river is so much in the grip of

Beaulieu Church

hydro-electric schemes that the nature of the stream has totally changed.

Anyone who enjoys vast sweeps of water, and the walls of dams, may find the road to Argentat very interesting, but along the twelve miles from Beaulieu to Argentat lies some of the most beautiful scenery in the Dordogne valley. We can follow this road up to Argentat, and then head west through the Causse de Martel to the busy little town of Brive-La-Gaillarde, a centre for the *causse* country.

10 The Causse Country

Not everyone likes rivers and their enclosing valleys. The river country has many admirers and a wide choice of delights, but those who crave the high plateaux and the windswept open fields can find a complete and invigorating change of scene in the causse country, here in the province of Quercy, between the Dordogne and the Lot.

The word 'causse' means a plateau, and these, the 'Moyennes Causses' lie like steps in a ladder astride the Dordogne river, to the east of the *département.* They are, from the north, the Causse de Martel, the Causse de Gramat and, below Cahors, the Causse de Limogne. These are the 'middle causses', smaller than the Grandes Causses of Larzac and Sauveterre in Lozère, but no less beautiful.

The causses are a result of the upheaval which created the Massif Central and the subsequent action of the major rivers, which in making their way down through the rock, cut out deep valleys to their river bed. The causses are best imagined as the fingers projecting from a clenched fist, where the knuckles are the central spine of the Massif. When the Massif arose, in primeval times, it tilted the whole of this land sideways to the west, and the rivers that now rise in the Massif run south-west to the Atlantic. As mentioned before, the true level of the land is on the causse. One goes *down* to the river rather than *up* to the plateau, and although the rivers have created much beauty as they carved their way down to the valley floor, they have left a lot of beauty behind them on the heights.

The limestone of the causses is porous and there are few streams. The water soaks into the rock and collects into underground rivers and grottoes, like the one at Le Grand Roc, and the one we have already visited at Padirac. Lacking surface water, the causse is a dry, bare country. The bones of the land lie close to the surface of the earth, breaking through in places to lie in strips, like grey ribs and knuckles on the surface of the fields. Every rainstorm washes rocks to the surface and these have been painfully collected off the fields and built into the drystone walls that edge the farmland. Agriculture, usually sheep or arable farming, continues to dominate the region and the usual walnut trees, though a little smaller now, still grow on the scanty earth, interspersed with dwarf oaks and the tangy sweet-smelling bushes of the *garrigue.*

From up on the causse, the traveller looks down across the deep blue-green valleys to the rivers far below, with the tall limestone cliffs rearing up from the trees clinging on either side. It is spectacular country. The roads across it swoop up and down, and around and over, surging about as they gain height on the one hand and lose it again on the other,

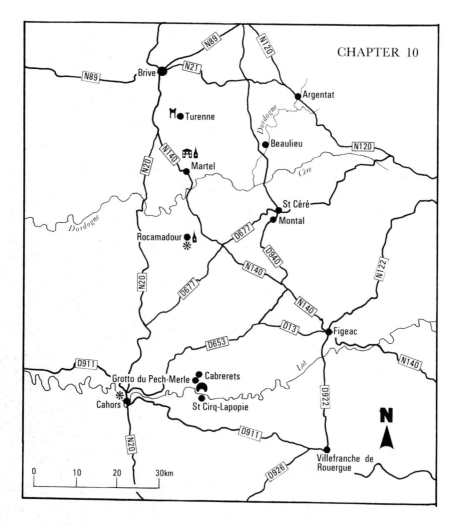

and the views are far and wide.

From the north, the traveller can swoop on the causse country from Brive-la-Gaillarde, that underrated little town, better known as a stop on the road to Spain than an attraction in its own right. South from Brive, on minor roads, which climb steadily up the smoother north face of the Causse de Martel, the traveller soon sees across the valley the crowded hilltops of

Turenne, where the Tower of Caesar on the castle prods an index finger at the sky. Little Turenne reeks of war and gave its name and title to the great French soldier Louis XIV's Marshal, the Vicomte de Turenne.

Henry de la Tour d'Auvergne, the first great soldier of the family, was a captain of Henry of Navarre, and commanded the Huguenot forces in the Limousin. It was his grandson, another Henry, that worked

The Tower of Caeser, Turenne

wonders in Flanders for Louis XIV, winning battle after battle in the 'War of Devolution'. Honours and wealth were heaped upon him, and he left a fortune in gold and honour to his family when he was buried at

Turenne

PLACES TO VISIT FROM CAHORS

Cabrerets
An old village on the Celé, a tributary of the River Lot. See the old Castle of the Devils. (The 'devils' were the English).

Marcilhac-sur-Celé
A medieval village, with ancient walls, a ruined abbey and tall towers.

St Cirq-Lapopie
Fine village with a fortified church, and fine views across the Lot.

Espagnac-Ste Eulalie
Old village. Caves nearby have Magdalenian paintings.

Cahors
Vineyards Tour. Cross Pont Valentré and then follow the river towards château of Mercuès (now an hotel) across the vineyards. Many '*degustations*', (tasting stations) along the way.

St Denis, among the kings and heirs of France, but from this high point the fortunes of the family disappeared, and in the next century they were forced to sell their lands at Turenne to the Crown. Their properties were bought by Louis XV for over four million pounds, a sum in modern value almost beyond computation, but the decline continued. One of the sprigs of this house, Nicolas, later fought a famous duel at the Rond Pont des Champs-Elysées with that notorious rake, Giacomo Casanova, and somewhat to his surprise, lost, receiving a thrust in the thigh. He might have guessed that anyone with Casanova's gift for outraging husbands would be deft with a rapier.

The castle and town of Turenne date from the sixteenth century, and

they present excellent examples of the buildings, noble and humble, of the period. The Tower of Caesar is older than the rest of the castle and dates from the thirteenth century. Needless to say, it has nothing to do with the great Julius but many great buildings of the Middle Ages were given some lordly title and anything as outstanding as Turenne's great tower justifies a noble name.

South of Turenne, across the causse, lies the town of Martel, from which the causse itself takes its name. Martel is a magnificent little town, much steeped in history and named after the great Charles Martel who, after defeating the

Saracens at Poitiers in AD 732, pursued their army south and finally broke them near the spot on which Martel now stands. Charles founded the church of St Maur here to commemorate his victory. The word Martel means hammer, and the arms of Charles Martel, with three hammers, are shown in relief over one of the doors of his church. St Maur is a fine building set deep in the town, surrounded, as in medieval times, with cobbled courtyards and alleys. The tympanum over the main door is particularly striking, showing Christ in glory, surrounded by angels with trumpets. Inside, the church retains much of its medieval wall painting, and is well worth inspecting.

Nearby is the Hotel de la Raymondie, built in the thirteenth century by the Turenne family, and now the town hall and tourist office. The local people give the name of 'Henri Curt Mantel' to the eldest son of King Henry II of England. But though he met his end here, this is incorrect.

Henry II, called Plantagenet, Count of Anjou, was not King of England when he married Eleanor of Aquitaine. Stephen of Blois still ruled England, but he died shortly after Henry and Eleanor were married, and the couple rode rapidly north to claim this addition to their already extensive lands. Fresh from his nuptials, Henry arrived in England wearing new clothes, including, in the then fashionable French style, a short cape which hung from his shoulders to his waist. His English nobles, who wore the long, floor-length cloaks so necessary in their draughty northern castles, were much amused at this

impractical southern garment, and nicknamed Henry, 'Curt-Mantel' or 'short cloak'. This name was in common use years before young Henry was even born. In the idiom of the time he should correctly be called Henry Fitz-Henry, but in 1170 Henry II, seeking to ensure the peaceful succession of his House, had his son, young Henry, crowned and made the nobles swear loyalty to him as their lord; so there were then two King Henrys. This meant that the nobles were put in a difficult position when, as eventually happened, the two kings fell out, for having sworn loyalty to both, which one should the nobles follow in battle? Moreover, how should they differentiate between the two King Henrys? The people at the time called him simply the Old King and the Young King, and where or when subsequent generations transferred the Old King's nickname to his son is not known. Henry, (the Young King) died here in agony and remorse after sacking the shrine at Rocamadour in 1183.

Martel is also the centre for the manufacture of that *eau de noix* mentioned in the previous chapter, which can be sampled at various points in the town, and one can tour the ramparts and the seven *tours* for which the town is noted, and take a little refreshment gratis while doing so. The *dégustations,* or tasting shops, are most generous with their samples, and it often takes considerable resistance and self-control to avoid having too much. The method is shrewd, for even those who go in only to taste usually come out with a bottle. Like the *eau de prunes, eau de noix* is an acquired taste, but very palatable.

From Martel it is only a short distance across the Dordogne and through Montvalet to the spectacular pilgrimage site of Rocamadour, on the Causse de Gramat. The little town lies in the deep valley of the River Alzou, and its first sight as it clings to the cliff-face in the far side of the ravine is enough to take the breath away. Rocamadour is, by repute, the second most beautiful town in France, with Mont St Michel the first.

It is difficult to imagine anyone building a place like Rocamadour today, for the town is situated on one side of a gigantic ravine and seen from across the void, the town seems to hang in mid-air, unsupported. It is reached by climbing down through a tunnel, then out and round the head of the valley and finally down again to the

town. The visitor enters through the fortified main gate, and is at once in a medieval pilgrimage city. On either hand are the shops and stalls of tradesmen, while on the right tower the walls of the pilgrimage church. From the road the Staircase of the King, which the pilgrims would climb painfully on their knees, labours towards the shrine of the Virgin. Each pilgrim carried a candle, and candles are still on sale at the foot of the staircase because some of the pilgrims who still come to Rocamadour feel that only the old ways will attract the attention and compassion of the Virgin.

At the top of the stairs, past a little museum and a number of smaller churches and chapels, lies the object of all this veneration, the Virgin of Notre Dame de Rocamadour, and few places can still retain such a timeless air as this little chapel. The visitor enters, a little blinded by the bright sunlight, and sees before him in their holders, ranks of tall, white, smoking candles. The ceiling above is caked black with soot from centuries of such candle smoke, and high up are the chains and manacles of prisoners, (for the Virgin of Rocamadour was a patron of prisoners), who prayed for their release and brought their fetters to Rocamadour when they obtained it. Today, trinkets adorn the walls, for Rocamadour is no empty shrine. Pilgrims still come, and if their prayers are answered, they sometimes bring mementoes or votive offerings as an encouragement to others. Swords, ship-models, medals, and insignia of honour hang in their places around the walls, while from her niche in the corner the Virgin watches the door with an engaging gaze. This is a 'Black Virgin', blackened by time and carved by some unknown medieval craftsman. She is probably about eight hundred years old and in her time has seen emperors and kings, saints, and many unrepentant sinners kneel at her feet.

The Virgin of Rocamadour has always had a special sympathy for soldiers. In the Middle Ages knights called here to pray for her assistance in the fulfilling of some particular vow. Her shrine in those days was full of shattered lances, swords and armour, all the trappings of war. Legend has it that the Paladin Roland, who rode through here on his way to fight the Saracens at Roncesvalles, pledged that his sword, Durandal, should be placed in the shrine after his death, and so it was. Unfortunately for the story,

Roland was killed centuries before the grave of St Amadour was discovered at Rocamadour, but the sword at least eventually found its way there, or so the story goes.

It was the Virgin's reputation as a friend of soldiers which brought great disaster to her shrine, for in 1183, Henry (the young king), in rebellion as usual against his father, rode down on Rocamadour and stole the treasure of the Virgin to pay his *routiers*. He even took Roland's sword from the chapel, and rode off north with it hanging by his side. This was an act of sacrilege, and writs of anathema and excommunication would surely have caught up with the young king, had not a more final fate — or perhaps the Virgin's vengeance — overtaken him. When only a few miles away from the shrine, he was struck with a sudden illness and, unable to ride, he was taken to Martel and lodged in the Maison Fabri, where a few days later he died. Of all his following, only one man, the knight William the Marshal, remained with him, and the young king died in the ashes on the floor of his lodgings.

When the young king sacked it in the twelfth century, Rocamadour was already one of the great shrines of Christian Europe, ranking with the great shrine of St James at Santiago de Compostela, and immensely rich. There was no great event or miracle to start the cult which brought the pilgrims, but at some time in the eleventh century, some monks excavating for a cell, discovered a coffined body. It may have been that of an early anchorite monk, but the monks who discovered it declared it to be the body of Zaccarias, a follower of Christ

Le Pont Valentré, Cahors

and friend of Mary. The trickle of visitors soon grew to a flood, and the shrine of Amadour, the friend of Mary, was quickly established. It was probably one of those early pilgrims who brought the statue of the Virgin, about which miracles were soon reported, but as at Cadouin, relics bring wealth, and miracles make wonderful publicity.

Modern man finds the idea of the pilgrimage and the veneration of relics, evidence of the rather foolish attitude that our simpler forefathers had to the after-life. Living in a well-travelled world, we know that there are enough pieces of the True Cross to build Noah's Ark and enough pieces of Noah's Ark to build sufficient ships to save all the inhabitants of Sodom and Gomorrah. Medieval man had no such information to undermine his faith, but he had faith also in the beneficial effects of the pilgrimage, and the veneration of relics in this life and in Heaven afterwards, and the cult of the pilgrimage continues today and, as at Lourdes, can even flourish.

In medieval times no king's treasure was complete without a comprehensive stock of relics. This collection of relics, or 'halidom' as it was called, proved the king's piety, gave him something to turn to in hours of need, and came in handy for the swearing of powerful oaths. All Englishmen remember how Earl Harold was tricked by William of Normandy into swearing to support his claim to England on a box of holy relics. Relics were widely collected, and it is recorded that when Fulk Nerra, Count of Anjou, who had led a life of quite surpassing wickedness, went to Jerusalem to pray for forgiveness, he was so keen to obtain a piece of the Holy Shrine for his *halidom* that he bit off a chunk with his teeth!

The Virgin of Rocamadour is a curious relic of a simpler age, and few people can visit her chapel and not wonder at the power she has exerted on Christian pilgrims for centuries. Rocamadour lies in the *département* of Lot and is today an almost totally commercialised tourist centre. Tourists are, after all, the pilgrims of the twentieth century, and they probably, on balance, bring more blessings than they receive. They certainly throng the streets of Rocamadour and spend heavily before pouring back through the main gate to climb into their coaches and depart. Those who stay will enjoy the Hotel de l'Ascenseur, or the Lion d'Or.

Rocamadour lies in a great fissure of our second causse, the Causse de Gramat, which lies between the Dordogne and her southern sister, the River Lot. Heading out of Rocamadour to the south, we pass over the high plateau of the Causse, and on to the little town with a name like a trumpet call, Labastide Murat! Joaquin Murat was one of the twenty-six Marshals created by Napoleon, and the finest leader of light cavalry the world has ever seen. Dressed in the gorgeous uniforms of his own design, Murat led charges that smashed the armies of Europe from the path of the Emperor. There is a museum in the town which commemorates the exploits of this hero.

Murat's parents kept an inn in the town, and were quite disappointed when their son joined the army in 1788. After serving in Napoleon's brilliant campaigns in Italy, Murat soon distinguished himself, went on the fateful expedition to Egypt and a few years later he married Napoleon's sister, Caroline. His advance was thereafter rapid and he eventually became, under Bonapartist patronage, the King of Naples. After the defeat at Waterloo, however, his decline was

La Rocque Gageac and the Dordogne river

Belcastel

Rocamadour

as rapid as his rise had been. He was driven from Naples by the returning Bourbons, and in attempting to re-capture his kingdom he was taken prisoner by the Neapolitans and shot.

South again now, down the valley of the River Vers, which has cut a deep fissure in the Causse, to the banks of the wide Lot itself, where we turn towards Cahors. Throughout our tour of the Dordogne, Cahors has featured on every signpost, sometimes near and sometimes further away, but always there and serving now as the finishing point for our trip through the rivers and hills of the Dordogne region. Cahors is not to be explored this time, but there is one sight still to be seen on this journey before we end it and turn for home. The Pont Valentré, a beautiful towered bridge, spans the Lot at Cahors and takes the road south.

This fine bridge marks the furthest extent of travels in the now popular Dordogne. The remainder of the book concentrates on that most neglected aspect of travelling, finding a different route which will, with a little care, lead back to the starting-point on less frequented routes; routes which also lead to some fresh and beautiful corners in the countryside of France.

11 Across the Charente

There is a saying that, wherever you are travelling to, getting there is half the fun; this philosophy can be extended to getting home again, by a different route, still on minor roads and, if possible, at a leisurely pace. The traveller who hangs on at his holiday destination until the last moment is faced with a hurried, tiring drive home, and probably arrives back in urgent need of another holiday. A leisurely return avoids this fate, and can provide unexpected benefits in terms of previously-undiscovered places of interest.

When you consider that it lies south of the popular Vendée, and north of the Dordogne, it is surprising that the region of Charente-Maritime is so neglected, and his only now creeping into the thoughts of committed travelling Francophiles. Perhaps it has just been lucky to escape the tourist hordes so far.

In fact, the Charente slipped out of the mainstream of French history during the time of Richelieu and the Wars of Religion. It was then a stronghold of the Protestant faith and the scene of many conflicts, notably at Jarnac and La Rochelle. Those wars, with much subsequent neglect, has left the area with many small towns and few big cities, a multitude of castles and plenty of variously-damaged churches, all washed by the soft Atlantic winds, and well worth more than a fleeting glance. The route lies west, round

Périgueux again, past Bourdeilles and Brantôme, before veering off the outward route and coming into the Charente through Riberac and Chalais.

Chalais is a town in two parts; the modern section on the banks of the Tiede, and the much more attractive old quarter on the little hill above. This little town contains a useful introduction to one of the discreet pleasures of the Charente, Romanesque architecture, which is abundant hereabouts.

The origin of the term Romanesque is subject to argument. Some say that although there is no direct link with the Romans, it takes the name and motivation from the classically severe Roman lines; others say the term comes from the flowing or 'Romantic' lines and tracery with which these otherwise plain buildings are decorated. Whatever the origin of the name, the Romanesque style is attractive. In Britain the Romanesque style is referred to as Norman.

The style evolved about the year AD1000 and flourished for about two hundred years until it was gradually replaced by the Gothic. The Romanesque attempted to create new and very large churches, which reflected the spirit of the age, but without really dealing with the structural problems confronting large buildings in the early medieval period; so they tended to collapse.

The problem was how to bridge the roof, or vault. To span the width the roof had to be heavy, and the walls supporting it had therefore to be thick, but on a low-pitched roof the weight pushes outwards, against the walls, and unless these were very strong, they were sure to topple. It took two hundred years and the influence of Archbishop Suger, the architect of St Denis, to show medieval builders that if the roof angle was steep, then the weight of the roof pressed down rather than out, and walls could therefore be both higher and thinner; hence the Gothic, although this, too, usually required the support of the classic flying buttress.

All that lay ahead in AD1000, and yet the the spirit of the age called for a change. It had been widely believed that the world would end in the year 1000, and when the millenium passed with no worse event than the coming of the Vikings, people began to hope and look to the future — even if the walls of their new churches continued to collapse.

Man is a tenacious animal, and constant effort and experiment created a style which is now instantly recognisable as Romanseque; flat, shallow-pitched roofs, usually covered with tiles rather than slate, thick walls, small, narrow windows, and strong pillars within the dark interior. The style is plain, solid and resolute, the builders making up for any lack of architectural finesse by decorating these churches with rich carvings, statues, tracery and tympanums.

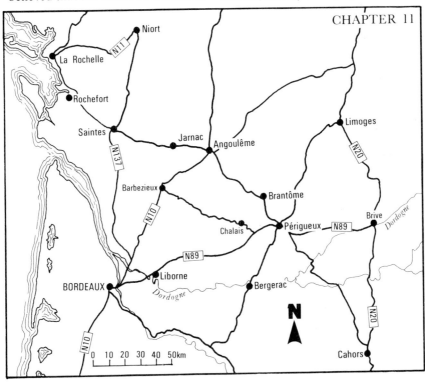

Here at Chalais, the Church of St Martial, just to the north of the town, is a typical example of the style. The façade is richly carved with scenes from the New Testament and has intricate tracery, even if all too many of the statues in the niches have their heads knocked off. The castle of Chalais, which gives good views over the town, once belonged to the Talleyrand family. One of them, for rebelling against Louis XIII, was executed at the orders of Cardinal Richelieu, who gave short shrift to any truculent noble, and they say it took thirty strokes of the axe to remove the poor man's head.

From Chalais, the road runs north and west still, through Brossac, skirting the Limousin which lies to the east, and heading for the town of Barbezieux, a very cheery little place and a good introduction to the Cognac country. Around here they produce the so-called 'petit champagne'; no wine this, but a cognac brandy and only that produced here and in the area around Cognac itself, 'la grande champagne', can truly be listed as 'Fine Champagne'; it is common for French people when ordering a brandy, to request not a cognac, but a 'fine'. That apart, the town produces glazed fruits and has a number of fine buildings, mostly medieval.

Jarnac on the River Charente is the town where in 1569, the great Condé, first leader of the Huguenots was killed in battle with the Catholic League, an event that marked the mid-point in the Wars of Religion. These began in 1562, when the Catholic Duc de Guise slaughtered some Protestants in Champagne, and went on until 1589, when Henry

of Navarre became Henri IV of France. The southern and western parts saw a great deal of the fighting, and such places as La Rochelle endured lengthy sieges, which destroyed both their medieval fortifications and much of their beauty. Even so, the towns remain historically interesting and are well preserved.

Jarnac, like many place hereabouts, is a centre for the cognac trade, with plenty of shops selling the local specific, and road lined with signs inviting travellers to stop in at the caves of Hine or Hennessey or Courvoisier, and sample a little of what they have to offer; not very good advice for the motorist. Hennessey seems to be the main producer of cognac hereabouts, and has a museum explaining the process of production, as well as vast which is said to contain the world's largest reserves of cognac. Cognac is produced from white grapes with an acid content high enough to induce fermentation without the addition of sugar or sulphur dioxide. The wine is distilled very slowly over a six-month period over open fires. After three years in casks the brandy is blended or decanted for further maturing in oak barrels, and most cognac brandies are aged between five and ten years before bottling.

Apart from brandy, one other worthwhile visit is to the cellars of the Château de Valois, all that is left of the medieval castle where François I was born. British prisoners captured during the Seven Years' War were incarcerated here and their scratchings and graffiti can still be seen on the walls.

From Cognac it is only a short

Château-Hostellerie near Cognac

distance of just over fifteen miles, to Saintes, in the western *départment* of Charente-Maritime. Saintes is a fine city and the largest town hereabouts. It was originally established by the Romans and has been a place of importance ever since. The old town lies on the south bank of the river, behind some seventeenth-century *quais,* and is a maze of narrow medieval streets and old houses, well worth wandering about in.

Niort is a good place to make an overnight stay, for two reasons. Firstly, it is a good centre for visiting the wetlands of the Marais-Poitevin, the *Venise-Verte,* the Green Venice (call it what you will), and secondly, it lies on the western arm of one of the pilgrim roads to Compostela, a route that must interest any historically-minded traveller.

That apart, it lies in Deux-Sèvres, the third of the four *départments* which make up the region of Poitou-Charentes, the others being Charente, Charente-Maritime and Vienne.

There is a direct road, and even an autoroute (the A10), leading up towards Niort from Saintes, but our chosen path follows minor roads and as always, this choice has hidden benefits because by following the D121 through Matha, it leads to Aulnay, which possesses one of the finest Romanesque churches in the area, and one which lies on the Road to St James at Compostela.

The Church of St Peter at Aulnay stands in the centre of a vast cemetery well studded with cypress trees, but it is not a gloomy place. It is too beautiful for that. On the left

PLACES TO VISIT AROUND COGNAC

Cognac Cellars or Chais
Martell, Hine, Courvoisier, in and around the town. Details from the *Syndicat d'Initiative.*

Église St Léger
Romanesque church in Cognac.

Château de Richemont, 3 miles to the east on N141.

Église St Etienne, Macqueville, 10 miles north-east of Cognac. Romanesque church in village.

Château de Valois
Interesting cellars

of the main door, among a series of rich carvings, is one depicting the crucifixion of St Peter who, although sentenced to be crucified, refused to die as his Lord had done, and was therefore nailed to the cross upside down. Other carvings show the wise and foolish Virgins, the Three Virtues overcoming the Three Vices, and angels adoring the Holy Lamb, as well as the signs of the zodiac and the work of the seasons. In medieval times, when most of the congregation were illiterate, these carvings served the clergy as illustrations of the life of Christ and the teachings of the Bible. Indeed, such carvings were often called 'The Bibles of the Poor', a daily, visible reminder of the gospels. Aulnay is a delightful spot, especially on a bright summer morning, with few people about. The road north leads to Niort, which is the capital of

Deux-Sévres and a sizable town with a population of about sixty thousand. Niort is one of those ideal little cities, so common in rural France, so rare in other countries, with flowers filling window boxes down all the streets, flags, fluttering from public buildings and an atmosphere of placid industry and quiet prosperity. The town received its first charter as a market from Eleanor of Aquitaine in 1203, when she had long been married to Henry II of England; and Henry and his son Richard both came here and added towers to the original castle, towers which still stand. After the Wars of Religion, when Niort, like most towns hereabouts, was considerably knocked about, it grew to fresh prosperity as a centre for the fur trade in pelts imported from Canada, and then as a textile centre. Today, while still a centre for the local farmers, it is chiefly noted among visitors as a touring centre for the Venise-Verte.

FOOTPATHS IN CHARENTE-MARITIME

GR4
From Cognac to Saintes and Royan.

GR36
Niort to Aulnay and along the Charente.

GR48
Along the River Vienne.

GR360
A tour of the Romanesque churches in Saintogne.

Tympanum of St Peter, Aulnay

The Venise-Verte, the Green Venice, is a tourist name, dreamed up by the local *Syndicat d'Initiative* to promote this curious fen, one of the largest and wildest wetlands in Western Europe, and known locally, and more correctly, as the Marais Poitevin, or simply, the Marais. The Marais lies between the Vendée to the north and the Aunis woods on the south, the sea on the west, and has its apex near Coulon, about six miles from Niort. It covers an area of some 1,500sq miles and is threaded by several rivers, most notably the Sèvre.

The Marais has always been a curious place, a vast, low-lying marsh, flooded by the sea on the one hand, and by the regular overflowing of the rivers on the other. Cistercian monks, who always choose remote spots for their work, came to live here in the thirteenth century, and though decimated by malaria, they began to dig ditches and canals, and build locks to control the periodic surges of river and tide. The monks intended to drain the Marais and transforms it into fertile farmland, and in this at least, succeeding generations have been partially successful. Part of the Marais is now cultivated as market gardens, growing cash crops of courgettes, artichokes and beans. Fishing for pike and perch and also eels is thriving, but above all this is a centre for dairy farming, with lush grass constantly available in the water meadows.

As a glance at even a small scale map will quickly reveal, the Marais is now a patchwork, or rather a chessboard of little fields, each surrounded by a deep ditch or a drainage canal. On these waterways, wide or narrow, small flat-bottomed boats are propelled by poles or

PLACES OF INTEREST IN SAINTES

Cathedral of St Pierre
Gothic and Romanesque, Place du Marché.

Musée des Beaux Arts, rue Victor Hugo.

The Old Town (Vieille Ville)
Maze of fascinating narrow medieval streets.

Église Ste Marie
Built in style of Saintogne-Romanesque.

paddles and these boats, or *plattes,* provide the only real way to explore the Marais. The local guide books say that the Marais is the Kingdom of the Punts. There are few roads, and anyway, the *plattes* have created a way of life as much as a mode of transport. The locals use the *plattes* to carry produce to market, cows to pasture, brides to church, or even visitors to the Marais to enjoy the peace and silence of the Gallic fen, and watch the birds.

Coulon, at the tip of this wetland, a few miles west of Niort, is the best centre for exploring the Marais, but there are *plattes* for hire at most of the little villages and a morning here is a delightful way to pass the time. A little poling or paddling is the ideal way to build up an appetite for lunch, and as one useful by-product of the tourist trade which is still largely French, the little villages of the Marais are well supplied with good restaurants. Local dishes include *cuisses de grenouilles* — frogs' legs; *mojettes a la Marichine*

— a dish based on beans; *matelotte d'anguilles* — fried and stewed eels, and good cheeses and cheese *tartes.*

La Rochelle, old port and fortress town, provides another excellent stopping place on a homeward route. The old port, which is the true heart and centre of this picturesque and charming town, dates from the Middle Ages, and yachts still enter between two towers, the Tour St Nicolas and the Tour de la Chaine, from which, as the name implies, a strong chain used to be lowered to prevent ships entering or leaving. Behind this, in the centre of the town, there is now a vast marine and *quais* for fishing boats, the perfect foreground for visitors lunching or dining at restaurants across the road.

La Rochelle has had a long and warlike history from medieval times and has belonged to England at least twice in that time. In 1573 it became a stronghold for the Huguenots, and was therefore besieged by the Catholic Duc d'Anjou, who later became that effeminate Henri III.

PLACES OF INTEREST AROUND NIORT

The Marais Poitevin
The *Venise Verte* (Coulon). Fascinating wetlands, home of much interesting wildlife.

Château de Couldrey-Salbant, Salbant, 4 miles north of Niort.

St Etienne la Cigogne, on N138, 5 miles south of Beauvoir. Romanesque church.

The duke besieged La Rochelle for six months, losing 20,000 of his men before retreating, and it remained in the hands of the Protestants after Henry IV issued the Edict of Nantes, which ceded such places as refuges for followers of the Protestant faith. In the next reign, Richelieu saw La Rochelle's prosperity and independence as a threat to his idea of a united France, and he persuaded Louis XIII to attack the town, during which the Cardinal himself donned armour and served the siege guns. Attempts to lift the siege, notably by the English Duke of Buckingham, were unsuccessful, and when the town finally fell in 1628, less then 5,000 of the original 27,000 men were still alive. The rest had fallen to wounds or starvation, but somehow or other the Protestant faith lived on here even after the Revocation of the Edict of Nantes and the expulsion of the Huguenots, so that until today, La Rochelle still contains a significant Protestant congregation.

In World War II, the nearby port of La Pallice sheltered the German battleship, the *Scharnhorst,* and the elements of the U-boat fleet, before Allied bombing drove them away, but in spite of many air attacks, La Rochelle survived virtually intact and is, a wonderful town to explore. The centre of the town lies along the Grande Rue des Merciers, and the Town Hall has a medieval façade and medieval battlements. From here, those who, enjoy prowling about old cobbled streets, can wander in almost any direction, with every road leading eventually back to the harbour where the smell of the sea gets stronger as the tide goes out and then rain patters in from the

---

PLACES OF INTEREST IN LA ROCHELLE

Old Harbour and towers of La Chaine and St Nicolas.

Église St Sauveur

Cathedral St Louis and **Hôtel de Ville.**

Rue des Merciers
Old houses.

---

west to send the late revellers home to bed.

There is a lot to be said for a swift look at somewhere new, not least because it can eliminate the more obvious places from a future trip, while showing the traveller a glimpse of what might be discovered on another visit off the beaten track. For instance those who want to see more of that classic Romanesque architecture should be sure to explore the Saintonge; but on the way north there can be few better routes than the one described here, which gives a good taste of yet another varied region and puts the traveller within two days comfortable and interesting drive of at least three Channel ports.

Clearly this area of Poitou-Charente deserves a visit in its own right, for not only is it an attractive region, but today it can boast a strong claim to fame on some solid historical pillars; an intricate descent from Roman times, fine examples of the Romanesque, a beautiful coast and hinterland, and the unique Marais — not at all a bad set of inducements.

12 Back to the Channel

Parthenay ought to be a mecca for travel writers, or even amateur travellers. It is a pleasant town anyway, the gateway into Poitou and Charente from the north, but in the eleventh century a Cluniac monk, Ameri Picaud, lived here, and although he was never canonised, he has some claim to being if not the patron saint, at least the founding father of the travel writing trade.

Ameri Picaud was a well-travelled cleric, who made the pilgrimage to St James of Santiago de Compostela some time in the first half of the twelfth century, and subsequently wrote about it in part of a manuscript, the *Codex Calextinus,* a five volume work, which records the life and legends of St James. Picaud certainly edited the *Codex,* and his travel writing, the *Liber Sancti Jacobi,* was not only the world's first guide book, but is also still in print, in Latin and French, which says something for both the book and the pilgrimage, which are still going strong after over eight hundred years.

Picaud was in orders at the monastery of Parthenay-le-Vieux, which stands, pure Romanesque, on a small hill on the right bank of the River Thouet. The monks came here originally from La Chaise-Dieu in the Auvergne, and that remote monastery has survived the ages rather better then Parthenay-le-Vieux, for the façade is much eroded, although there is one splendid carving of a mounted knight, hawk on fist, and

yet another of Melusine, the devil's daughter; not the most likely carving for the House of God one might think, but then medieval craftsmen has a fairly free hand in their choice of subjects.

During the Middle Ages, Parthenay was a major stop on the Western pilgrim road through France to Compostela, which led to the Gironde, south across the Landes and so to the Pyrénées, and it was probably the constant passing of pilgrims which gave Picaud the idea for his book. The pilgrims would rest in Parthenay for a day or two, before setting out across Poitou, crossing the Thouet by the gate and bridge of St Jacques, which still stand, a most splendid and well preserved example of a medieval bridge and gateway.

From Parthenay the traveller can make up time with a quick drive up the D938 to Thouars, then up through the rose-growing country to Doué-la-Fontane and up to the banks of the Loire at Gennes, from where a minor road leads west into Angers. Angers was the capital of the Plantagenet Counts of Anjou, and it has that certain air of a capital city, apart from having a fine castle on the banks of the Maine. The main Loire is five miles to the south but several rivers meet here, the Maine, the Sarthe, the Moyenne and the little Loir, so it is easy to get confused.

The big attraction here is the castle, which is vast, and dates from

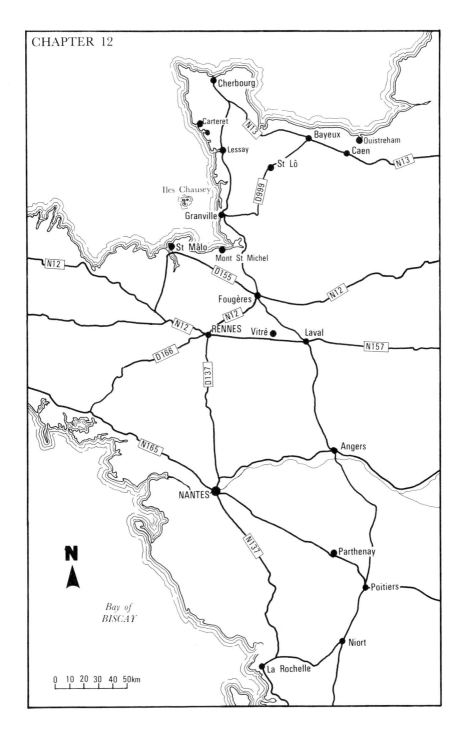

the thirteenth century, a creation not of the Plantegenets but of the Valois King, St Louis, who built it around 1220, after returning from the Holy Land. This is a concentric castle with seventeen round towers in over half a mile of curtain wall. Tapestries are on display here and in several other museums, notably the Logis du Roy and the Logis du Guiverneur. The cathedral is Gothic, and one of the windows shows scenes from the life of Thomas à Becket.

Once across the river Loire the land changes. I do not mean that is less attractive, but it is different, and in some ways far less French. The vineyards, the red-tiled roofs, and the soft airs of the south are now a long way behind, for this is Mayenne, and we are heading north, to the more familiar landscapes of Normandy, but through some fine places, notably the town of Laval, which is probably well worth a stop for those with a day or two to spare. To get there, take the minor route up the Mayenne from Angers through the village of Trappe du Port Salut. The famous Port du Salut cheese was made here until 1960, but the manufacture has been transferred to nearby Entrammes, although visitors can still buy cheese from the monks. The old town on the west surrounds the Vieux Château and is full of the old streets, while across the bridge of the Pont Vieux lies the much restored Romanesque cathedral, which probably best seen at distance. The other church, Notre Dame d'Avenières, has windows by Max Ingrand, while the castle contains, among other exhibits, paintings by Henri Rousseau, who was born in

PLACES TO VISIT IN AND AROUND PARTHENAY

Abbey of St Pierre, Parthenay-le-Vieux, 1 mile west on D743. Romanesque abbey.

Pont St Jacques
Excellent example of medieval fortified bridge-gate over river.

Rue de la Vaux - St Jacques
Street full of old houses.

Laval in 1844.

Laval is the capital of Mayenne and here the homeward-bound traveller has a choice. It is possible to head a little west, through Vitré and up to Fougères, or lean a little eastwards and enter Normandy through the hilly country of the Suisse Normande. Both routes have a lot to recommend them. Vitré and Fougères are fortress cities of Brittany, guarding the old march with France. Vitré has more atmosphere, a hilltop town with narrow, cobbled streets, leaning buildings and a great square fronting on to a vast, gaunt castle. If you like castles, a visit to Vitré is a must.

From here, a small road, the D178, leads after twenty miles to Fougères, more modern, often crammed with traffic but endowed with a very fine and well-preserved castle, which lies surrounded by a moat at the foot of the hill on which much of the town is laid out. The castle dates from 1173, and was built, or rather rebuilt, by Raoul de Fougères, the local lord after Henry II of England had destroyed the

PLACES TO SEE IN ANGERS

Castle of the Dukes of Anjou
Enormous well-preserved castle, with museums containing excellent tapestries.

Castle of St Maurice
Twelfth- and Thirteenth-century Gothic. Good stained glass.

La Corniche Angevin
Good views over the Loire and Mayenne from N751 west of Angers.

previous structure. The thirteen towers along the walls are a later addition. There are *son-et-lumière* shows here on summer evenings, and if one is on offer, it is well worth stopping the night to see it.

This route has further popular attractions to its credit, for by heading north again from Fougères, the traveller will soon come to Pontorson; a short distance up the causeway from there will will bring the traveller to Mont-St-Michel, which now lies in Normandy, to the distinct chagrin of the Bretons. The frontier between Normandy and Brittany is the River Cousenon (pronounced Quay-non), and for centuries this river flowed out to sea round the eastern side of Mont-St-Michel. Then a violent storm and high tides scoured out a new channel, the river flowed down the western side — as it still does — and historic, remarkable Mont-St-Michel came into the clutches of Normandy.

None of this need concern the present visitor, for whoever holds it, Mont-St-Michel is remarkable. It contains the shrine of St Michael, the archangel, who is usually commemorated in a pillar church, or one built on a high rock as here, or at Le Puy in the Auvergne. Monks built the first abbey here long before the Conquest of England, and in the centuries since the island has been a fortress, a prison and a pilgrim centre, held by the French and English in their turn until the end of the Plantagenet Wars. Today its it ranks as the *Premier Site de France,* the country's major tourist attraction, a decidedly mixed blessing.

From Easter until mid-September, Mont-St-Michel is a tourist-jammed hell, crammed with visitors and souvenir pedlars, and all is over-priced. If you can, go there out of season and preferably early in the day or at sunset. If a storm is blowing and the tide is sweeping in across the bay, so much the better, for at such times Mont-St-Michel, always striking, becomes truly dramatic.

Even in summer it is an essential photogenic spot, and those who contrive to climb up the winding, central street, to the top of 'La Merveille' and out onto the ramparts, will be fairly rewarded

PLACES TO SEE IN LAVAL

Musée du Vieux Château
Works by Henri Rousseau and folklore exhibits.

Église de Notre-Dame d'Avenières
Gothic-Renaissance church with modern stained glass.

with breathtaking views. The shrine
of St Michael is in a little chapel on
the right-hand side of the main
street, and those who do not care for
tourist junk can, by way of a
souvenir, purchase a replica of the
original pilgrim badge for a few
francs in the Tourist Office by the
main gate.

Following this route again offers
the traveller a choice. Turn west her
and you can take the Brittany Ferry
home to Portsmouth by St Malo and
the road to that historic port, the
City of Corsairs, leads via Cancale,
where the little restaurants on the
quay serve marvellous oysters. The
recommended route, however, is
towards Cherbourg, by staying hard
on the western edge of the Cotentin.

This road leads first to Granville,
another stout city, which has nice
views across the bay to Mont-St-
Michel, and flat against the
westering sky, the Iles Chausey, the
only Channel Islands which still
belong to France, even if they refer
to the remainder of the Channel
Islands as *Les Iles Anglo-Normandes.*

Coutances has been almost
entirely rebuilt in the last forty
years as the original city was
completely shattered in the fighting
of 1944. One survivor of that terrible
time is the Gothic cathedral, built
from about 1220, the most delicate
Gothic cathedral in Normandy, and
still preserving some of the original
thirteenth-century windows. Those
in the north transept show scenes
from the life of Thomas à Becket.

From Coutances, pick up the
minor road which runs along the
coast, to Lessay, for this route gives
fine views out to Jersey. Lessay, at
the mouth of the River Ay, has a
beautiful Romanesque abbey, but be
not deceived. The original, built in
1050, was knocked to pieces in 1944,
but rebuilt, using original tools on
original stone and as much of the
original fabric as could be gleaned
from the rubble. The result is
glorious and Lessay is well worth a
stop, especially during the second
weekend in September when the
town holds its Holy Cross Fair, an
event dating back to the Middle
Ages.

From here, minor roads lead on
to the mysterious little town of
Portbail, set in a wilderness of sand-
dunes; then to Carteret, a popular
seaside resort in summer; and then,
turning inland for the last time, to
Briquebec, where the town centre is
dominated by a vast castle, and
there, in the courtyard of the castle
is an hotel, built firmly into the
structure. *The Hotel de Vieux*

Chateau in Briquebec is a splendid place, once the seat of Robert de Briquebec, lieutenant of William the Conqueror — Queen Victoria slept here on a visit to France, and her bedroom still contains the contemporary furniture. The toilet, a little further down the same corridor, is built into the watchtower and illuminated by a arrow-slit!

Those who already know the Cotentin might prefer to take the eastern route from Laval, heading north up the D31 to Ernée and Gorron, into Normandy and up to the town of Domfront, gateway to the Suisse Normande. Domfront lies on an escarpment along the River Varenne, looking south to the *bocage* country, a maze of fields enclosed by high, thick hedges. The old castle is mostly in ruins, but the town has one excellent Romanesque church, the eleventh-century Notre-Dame-sur-l'Eau, which, as the name implies, is on the banks of the river.

Clécy, the next stop, is best known as a touring centre for the jumbled country of the Suisse Normande, but there is plenty to see in the town itself, the churches of Clécy and nearby Véy, the monastery at Pacey and, for it is a beautiful spot, the riverside near the Moulin de Véy.

Those who still have a day or two in hand could do a lot worse than base themselves at Clécy, and tour about. The city of Caen, capital of the Norman dukes is just over twenty miles to the north, and well worth half a day of anyone's time. The castle in the centre held Duke William's court at the time, although much enlarged and now the site of several museums, notably the Musée de Normandie. Nearby

Caen University, one of the finest in France, was founded in 1432 by John, Duke of Bedford, brother of Henry V, and Regent of France for the infant Henry VI.

Caen's two principal curiosities are the twin abbeys, the Abbaye aux Hommes built by William the Conqueror, and the Abbaye aux Dames, built Matilda, his wife. Both were built as an act of penance for the sin of consanguinity. William should not have married Matilda of Flanders since they were cousins, and the Pope excommunicated them on their wedding day, only lifting the ban when they agreed to build two abbeys as a sign of contrition. Matilda lies buried in the transept of her foundation, but although a slab marks the site of William's tomb in the Abbaye aux Hommes, the Conqueror's bones were dug up during the Revolution and thrown into the river.

Caen is a modern miracle, for it suffered terribly during the post-D-Day fighting of 1944, when the city was pounded by artillery and heavily bombed for weeks on end, and reduced to rubble. The same is true of many of these Norman cities, towns and villages; they are pleasant places today, embellished with trees, full of flowers in window boxes or hanging baskets, and to the casual eye, still rich in fine old buildings. A careful look will reveal the true extent of post-war reconstruction, and it says a great deal for the taste and stubbornness of the Norman people, that they have so successfully revived the beauty of their province after the savagery of war. Here for sure, 'grim-visaged war has smoothed his wrinkled front' and the result is to the credit

Moulin de Vey, Clecy

of the local poeple.

Travellers who came north as far as Caen have a choice of homeward ports, and can turn east to Le Havre or cross the Seine and the Pays de Caux to Dieppe, but Cherbourg is the closest and can be reached on a series of minor roads along the D-Day coast along the Bay of the Seine, or more directly through Bayeux.

Bayeux, unlike many Norman cities, was spared destruction in 1944, as it was captured swiftly on the evening of 6 June, the first French town to be liberated by the Allies. It is chiefly remembered by the English for the so-called Bayeux Tapestry, which the French call the *Tapisserie de la Reine Mathilde.* which is now on view in the Centre Guillaume le Conquerant in the centre of Bayeux. The Bayeux Tapestry is actually an embroidery, worked in England after the Conquest, probably by ladies of the old Saxon Court, for their needlework was famous. It was commissioned as a cathedral hanging by the Conqueror's brother, the warlike Bishop Odo of Bayeux, about 1080, although the first reference to its existence is in a cathedral inventory of 1476. The Tapestry is quite remarkable and is now beautifully displayed under glass. Seventy metres long and fifty centimetres wide, it records in detail the events leading up to the Conquest, and the invasion itself in over fifty scenes, although what happened after the Conquest when:

'Cold heart and Bloody hand
Now rule the English land'

is not part of the narrative.

Bayeux Cathedral is a thirteenth-century-Gothic structure, very impressive and in excellent preservation, as is the rest of the town centre where many beautiful medieval and later period houses lean towards each other across narrow, cobbled streets.

North of Caen, along the Bay of the Seine, lies the D-Day coast, and since war and stories of war have underpinned our travels in this book, it might be a fitting finish to conclude our travelling with a brief tour down this now peaceful stretch of coast, remarkable today, if at all, for an air of tranquillity.

Indeed, parked behind one of the beaches, looking down across the smoothly sloping sand to where the sea slops gently on the shore, it is hard to believe that anything ever really happened, here, on this spot and well within living memory, and yet it did.

Great armies came ashore here on

D-Day, 6 June 1944, great battles were fought, brave deeds were done and yet what few memorials remain. Those who have seen the old newsreels will recognise the house at St Aubin, where the Canadians and 48 Commando fought so bitterly to gain a foothold, and the iron girders of Pegasus Bridge astride the Caen canal are still scarred by bullets, but really the obvious signs of that cataclysmic struggle are very few — unless you look about with a keen eye, and a thoughtful mind.

The best way might be to begin outside Bayeux, with a visit to the British Military Cemetery, which contains the graves of five thousand men who died in the Normandy campaign. Then go south and east, to Caen and there turn north, along the canal, towards the port of Ouistreham; half way there the traveller will pass Pegasus Bridge, captured on the night of 5-6 June 1944 in a coup-de-main by glider forces of the British 6th Airborne Division. To the east, around Ranville, the rest of this great division landed to hold the flank of the invasion forces, while east of Ouistreham, where No 4 Commando spearheaded the assault, lies Sword Beach, where the British landed, then Juno, the Canadian area, then Gold, then bloody Omaha where the American infantry were cruelly handled in the surf, and so, round the corner of the bay to Utah and that little place we passed through on our outward journey, Ste-Mère-Eglise.

It pays, here as always, when travelling through France, to get out of the car and look about a bit, and those who do so will soon see that here at least, the events of 1944, if not brooded upon, are at least not forgotten.

There is a museum to the French troops of 4 Commando at Ouistreham, and plenty of plaques and memorials along the shore, at La Breche where No 3 Commando landed, in the shape of a Sherman tank in the square at Courseulles, dredged from the sea years after the battle, in the excellent D-Day Museum at Arromanches, which no visitor to these parts should miss, or over the hill and down to the little town of Port-en-Bessin, captured by (Royal Marine) Commando, who fought their way inland just to take this essential port from the rear.

West of here lies the American beach, Omaha, where the Big Red One, the US First Infantry Division, landed and were cut to pieces. Those who think that it was all so long ago, should visit the vast and beautiful US Military cemetery above St Laurent and note how young the men were who died here. Wars are fought by young men and over seven thousand lie here, above the beach they fought to capture and hold.

The path now lies homeward, either from Ouistreham where a new ferry crossing to Portsmouth has recently been introduced, or back to our starting point at Cherbourg, up the eastern coast of the Cotentin, by Utah Beach, to the little fishing port of St Vaast-la-Hougue, to Barfleur, to Cherbourg, the ferry, and the short voyage home.

PLACES TO VISIT ON THE D-DAY COAST

Pegasus Bridge
On Caen Canal.

British Military Cemetery
Bayeux.

Musée de Débarquement
(D-Day Museum) Arromanches.

Ouistreham
No 4 Commando beach.

La Breche
No 3 Commando beach.

Courselles
3rd Canadian Division beach.

St Aubin
48 (RM) Commando beach

Port-en-Bessin
No 47 (RM) Commando.

St Laurent
US Military Cemetery.

Omaha Beach
1st & 29th US Infantry beach.

Further Information

MUSEUMS

Archaeological Museum

In Château Eymet
Tel: M. Vautier on (53) 23 92 33
(home) or (53) 23 80 26 (office)
Open: Sunday afternoon subject to
prior appointment being made.
Collection housed in an annexe of
the château; paleontology,
archaeology, popular arts and
traditions.

The Doctor André Voulgre Museum of Art and Tradition

2 rue Raoul Grassin
Mussidan
Tel: (53) 81 23 55
Open: 15 June to 15 September,
daily (except Tuesday) 9.30am-12
noon and 2-6pm; rest of the year,
Saturday afternoon Sunday and
holidays; closed last two weeks of
September.

The Eugène Leroy Museum and the Museum of Old Périgord

Place Bertran de Born
Montignac
Tel: (Tourist Office) (53) 51 82 60
Open: 1 June to 15 September, daily
(except Sunday afternoon) 10am-12
noon and 3-6pm; rest of the year, by
appointment only.
Historical scenes showing life in old
Périgord. Also mementoes of the
novelist Eugène Leroy.

Fernand Desmoulin Museum

Abbaye
Brantôme
Tel: (Town Hall) (53) 05 70 21
Open: for two weeks at Christmas
and Easter.
Museum dedicated to the painter
Fernand Desmoulin.

Gallo-Roman Museum

Montcaret, 24230 Vélines
Montcaret
Tel: (53) 58 60 25
Open: 1 May to 30 September, daily
(except Tuesday) 9am-12 noon and
2-4.30pm; 1 October to 30 April,
museum closes at 4pm.
On a Gallo-Roman site: exhibits
consist of a large proportion of the
finds on the site.

Maison de la Truffe

Eco-Musée de Sorges
24420 Savignac-les-Églises
Sorges
Tel: (53) 05 90 11
Open: daily (except Tuesday) 2.30-
6.30pm.

Military Museum

32 rue des Farges
Périgueux
Tel: (53) 53 47 36
Open: daily (except Sunday and
holidays) 10am-12 noon and 2-6pm.
Over 20,000 exhibits: armour,
uniforms, weapons etc from the
Middle Ages to the present.

Municipal Museum
Town Hall, Place de la Liberté
Villefranche de Lonchat
Tel: (53) 80 77 25
Open: daily (except weekends and holidays) 8am-12 noon and 2-6pm.
Exhibits of regional pottery, carved wood, documents etc.

Musée des Pénitents Blancs
Rue Jean Jacques Rousseau
Sarlat la Canéda
Open: Easter to 10 October, Monday-Saturday 10am-12 noon and 3-6pm, Sunday 3-6pm.
A large number of religious objects — reliquaries, wooden statues and a remarkable stone *Pieta.*

Museum of Local Art
Saint Astier
For information contact the
Syndicat d'Initiative
Tel: (53) 54 13 85.

Museum of Périgord
22 cours Tourny
Périgueux
Tel: (53) 53 16 42
Open: daily (except Tuesday) 10am-12 noon and 2-5pm.
One of the greatest archaeological museums in France, with extensive collections ranging from prehistory in France, Africa and Scandinavia; Greek and Roman artefacts; Gallo-Roman exhibitions etc.

Museum of Popular Art and Traditions
Rue du Fond du Bourg, St Jean de Côle, 24800 Thiviers
Tel: (53) 55 30 24
Open: 15 June to 1 October, daily 10am-12 noon and 2-6pm; 15 February to 15 June and 1 October to 1 December, Sunday and holidays 2-5pm.
Remarkable collection of local implements and artefacts; reconstruction of an old tavern, house and bedroom.

Museum of Religious Art
Abbaye de Chancelade
Chancelade
Enquiries: Tourist office of Périgueux, Tel: (53) 53 44 35
Open: 15 June to 15 September, daily 2-6.30pm; at any other time by request.
Museum of objects of religious significance: priests, vestments, missals, chalices statues etc.

Museum of Weaving and of Traditions and Art
Château de Varaignes
24360 Piegut Pluviers
Varaignes
Tel: (53) 56 30 97
Open: daily 10am-12 noon and 2-5pm.

Museum of Wine and of Small Craft
5-7 Rue des Conferences
Bergerac
Tel: (53) 57 80 92
Write to the museum for information on opening times.

National Museum of Tobacco, and Local History Museum
Maison Peyrarède
Bergerac
Junction of rue des Rois de France, rue de l'Ancien Port and place du Feu.
Tel: (53) 57 60 22
Open: Tuesday-Friday 10am-12 noon and 2-6pm, Saturday 10am-12 noon and 2-5pm, Sunday 2.30-

6.30pm. Closed on bank holidays.
Museum of the history, culture and
industry of tobacco and its
associated products. Also the
history of the town in a collection of
documents, coins, archaeological
finds etc.

National Prehistory Museum
Château Eyzies
Les Eyzies de Tayac
Tel: (53) 06 97 03
Open: daily (except Tuesday)
9.30am-12 noon and 2-6pm;
December to February, museum
closes at 5pm.
Museum occupies the ruined
château. Large varied and
interesting collection of prehistoric
exhibits.

Paul Reclus Museum
Place de la Halle
Domme
Tel: (53) 28 37 09
Open: July and August, daily 10am-
12 noon and 3-7pm; April to June,
September and October, daily 10am-
12 noon and 3-6pm.
Collections of local prehistoric
finds; popular art and tradition; and
of the famous geographer Élisée
Reclus.

Speleology Museum
Fort du Tayac
Tel: M. Bouyssou (53) 59 12 86
Open: 15 June to 15 September,
daily (except Saturday) 9am-12
noon and 2-6pm. Other times by
request.

CHÂTEAUX

====

Château Baneuil
Baneuil 24150

Tel: (53) 61 08 31
Open: 1 July to 20 September, daily
(except Sunday) 10am-12 noon and
3-6pm.
Guided tours.

Château Beynac
Beynac 24220 (10km from Sarlat)
Tel: (53) 29 50 40
Open: 1 March to 15 November,
daily 10am-12 noon and 2.30-5pm.
Thirteenth-century castle, parking,
guided tours and information in
English available.

Château Biron
Biron 24540
Tel: (53) 22 62 01
Open: 1 February to 15 December,
daily (except Tuesday) 9-11.30am
and 2-6pm; July and August, daily.
Guided tours, English available in
July and August. Dances and
concerts held at the château.

Château Bourdeilles
Bourdeilles 24310, 10km from
Brantôme
Tel: (53) 05 73 36
Open: 1 February to 30 September,
daily (except Tuesday) 9-11.30am
and 2-6pm; July and August, daily.
Guided tours, brochure, English
available July and August. Concerts
and exhibitions of paintings.

Château les Bories
Antonne et Trigonant 24420, 11km
from Périgueux
Tel: (53) 06 00 01
Open: 1 July to 9 September, daily
10am-12 noon and 2-5pm. Rest of
the year on request.
Parking, brochure, English-speaking
guide.

Château de Breuilh
Nr St Antoine
Open: 1 May to 30 September,
Thursday, Saturday and Sunday 2-
6pm.
Extensive wine cellars.

Château Castelnau
Open: Easter to September, daily
(except Tuesday) 9am-12 noon and
2-6pm.

Château les Eyzies de Tayac
Les Eyzies de Tayac 24260
Tel: (53) 06 97 03
Open: 1 March to 30 November,
daily (except Tuesday) 9.30am-12
noon and 2-6pm; 1 December to 28
February, closes at 5pm.
Guided tour on demand (two weeks
notice required), explanatory panels,
brochure.

Château Fages
Open: Easter to mid-September,
daily (except Tuesday) 10am-12
noon and 3-6pm.

Château Fénelon
Sainte Mondane 24370
Tel: (53) 28 71 55 and 29 78 97
Open: 1 June to 30 September, daily
10am-12 noon and 2-7pm; 1 October
to 31 May, closes at 6pm.
Guided tours, brochure.

Château fort Grignols
Grignols St Astier 24110
Tel: (53) 54 25 40
Open: 1 June to 30 September, daily
(except Monday) 2.30-7pm. At other
times groups may be admitted on
request.
Guided tours. A visit of the grounds
is free.

Château Gageac
Rouillac 24240, 18km from Bergerac
Tel: (53) 27 92 82
Enquire locally for details of
opening times.

Château Hautefort
Hautefort 24390
(Mme de Bastard)
Tel: (53) 50 40 04
Open: Easter to 15 September, daily
9am-12 noon and and 2-7pm; 16
September to 2 November, daily
9am-12 noon and 2-6pm; 3
November to Easter, Sunday, and
holidays 2-5pm and for groups on
request.
Guided tours, English. Concerts and
temporary exhibitions held. Also
classical flower garden of the
seventeenth and eighteenth century,
in the grounds. Opening times as for
the château.

Château Jumilhac
Jumilhac le Grand 24630
Open: 15 March to 30 June, Sunday
and holidays 2-6pm; 1 July to 15
September, daily 10am-12 noon and
2-6.30pm; 15 September to 15
November, Sunday and holidays 2-
6pm.
Guided tours, brochures, English
guide. Concerts and plays held.

Château Lanquais
Lanquais 24150, 16km from
Bergerac
Tel: (53) 61 24 24
Open: 1 April to 31 October, daily
(except Thursday) 9.30-12 noon and
2.30-7pm.
Guided tours. Concerts and plays
held.

Château Les Milandes
Open: 1 April to 30 September, 9am-12.30pm and 2-7pm.

Château Monbazillac
Monbazillac 24240
Tel: (53) 58 30 27 and 57 06 38
Open: 1 May to 31 October, daily 9.30am-12 noon and 2-6.30pm; 1 November to 30 April, closes at 5.30pm.
Guided tours, English in July and August, brochures.

Château Montbrun
Verdon 24520
Tel: (53) 23 21 51
Open: on request only

Château de Montal
Open: 1 March to 31 October, 9am-12 noon and 2-5.30pm.

Château Puymartin
Marquay 24200
Open: 1 July to 15 September, daily 10am-12 noon and 2-6pm.
Guided tours of interior and grounds, English guide.

Château de Puyguilhem
On D83 north-east of Brantôme
Open: daily (except Tuesday) 10am-12 noon and 2-5pm.

Château La Treyne
Open: 15 March to 15 October, 8.30am-12.30pm and 2-7.30pm.

Château Verignac
Open: 1 July to 15 September, 10am-12 noon and 2-7pm.

Domme (Porte des Tours)
Domme 24250, 10km from Sarlat
Tel: (52) 28 31 83

Open: 1 June to 30 September, daily 11am-12 noon and 5-6pm; by request to groups during the rest of the year.
Guided tour, brochure.

Tour Mataguerre
Périgueux 24000
Open: on request only.
Guided tours, English guides, leaflets and plaques.

GARDENS

Jardin Botanique de Bordeaux
Terrasse du Jardin public
Place Bardineau
33000 Bordeaux
Tel: (56) 52 18 77
Open: daily 9am-dusk.
Large and varied botanical garden.

Jardin de Vayres
33870 Vayres
(Mme Dubost)
Tel: (56) 84 85 15
Open: Saturday, Sunday and holidays; winter, 2.30-5pm; summer, 2-7pm.
Beautiful formal gardens.

Parc Bordelais
Rue de Bocage
33000 Bordeaux Gauderan
Tel: (56) 90 91 60
Open: daily 7am-dusk.
28 hectares, 2,500 trees.

Parc de Marqueyssac
Vezac
24220 St Cyprien
(M & Mme de Jonghe d'Ardoye)
Open: 1 August to 30 September by prior arrangement only.
Garden designed by le Notre, panoramic views.

SHOW CAVES

Caverne ornée de Bara Bahau
24260 Le Bugue-sur-Vézère, 10km
from Eyzies
Tel: (53) 06 27 47
Open: Easter to end September,
daily 9am-12 noon and 2-6.30pm;
October, Sunday only.

Grotte préhistorique de Rouffignac
5km from Eyzies
Tel: (53) 05 41 71
Open: Easter to November, daily;
rest of year Sunday only.

Grottes de Fontirou
47340 Le Castella, between Agen
and Villeneuve-sur-Lot
Tel: (53) 70 32 35
Open: Easter to October, daily 8am-
8pm; October to Easter, Sunday and
by appointment only.

Grottes de Lacave
Lacave 46200, Souillac, between
Souillac and Rocamadour on the
D43
Tel: (65) 37 87 03
Open: Easter to end October, daily
9am-12 noon and 2-6.30pm.

Grottes de Villars
On D82 north of Puyguilhem
Open: 15 June to 15 September,
daily.

Padirac
Open: Easter to 15 October, daily.
Boat trip to see Stalactites and
Stalagmites.

La Roque St Christophe
Peysac-le-Moustier, 24620 Les
Eyzies
Enquiries: Syndicat d'Initiative es

Eyzies
Tel: (53) 06 23 22
Open: Easter to end September,
daily 9.30am-12 noon and 2-6.30pm.

Also many show caves and
prehistoric artefacts at Les Eyzies de
Tayac.

SPORTS AND LEISURE

Camping and Caravanning
Camping sites are plentiful and
practically every village now
possesses a properly appointed
camping site. Camping in farm
meadows and farmhouse self-
catering accommodation (gîtes
ruraux) are both good ways of
discovering the country life.
Details:
Féderation Française de Camping-
 Caravanning (FFCC)
78 rue de Rivoli, 75004 Paris
Telephone: 272 84 08

Fédération des Gîtes Ruraux
35 rue Godot-de-Mauroy 75009 Paris
Telephone: 742 25 43

Water sports
There are lakes both natural and
artificial on which bathing and
pleasure boating are now provided.
There is water-skiing in the Valley of
the Lot.

Riding holidays
Horseback excursions may be
enjoyed in the Limousin, Quercy,
Landes and Périgord.
Horse drawn caravans and
barouches may be hired in the
Quercy, Limousin, and Périgord.
Details:
Association Nationale du Tourisme

Equestre (ATNE)
15 rue de Bruxelles 75009 Paris
Telephone: 281 42 82

Rambling

Those who prefer walking will find blazed footpaths to take them all over the region.
Details:
Comité National des Sentiers de Grande Randonnée (CNSGR)
92 rue de Clignancourt, 75018 Paris
Telephone: 259 60 40

ZOOLOGICAL PARKS, NATURE RESERVES

Close des Sources Zoological Gardens

Regional and exotic animals (lynx, hyenas, eagles etc).

Le Thot

Park with animals at liberty (bison, European stags and does, mottled deer and tarpan horses).

FESTIVALS AND OTHER EVENTS

February
Bordeaux
Antiques Fair.

May
Bordeaux
International Music Festival and International Fair.
Chancelade
'Heures Musicales du Périgord'.

June
St Émilion
New Wine Festival.

June-July
Abbeys Festival.

July
Sarlat
Theatre Festival.
Bellac
National Music and Drama Festival.
Bonaguil
Music Festival.

August
St Jean-de-Côle
Chamber Music Concert.
Aquitaine Coast Music Festival.
Meyrals
'Musique à la Rougerie'.
Bonaguil
Craft Festival.

September
Bordeaux area
Ceremonial opening of the grape harvest.
Gourdon
Village Music Festival.

October
Limoges
Butchers' Festival.

November
Bordeaux
'Sigma' (contemporary arts festival).

TRAVELLING IN FRANCE

By Car
Driving
Keep to the right, overtaking on the left. Beware '*priorité à droit*' in towns. Drivers coming from the right, have right of way.

Speed limits
Built up areas 60km/h (37mph) unless otherwise indicated. Outside built up areas 90km/h (56mph) unless otherwise indicated. By-pass motorways 110 km/h (68mph). Dual carriageway roads with central reserve 110 km/h (68mph). Inter-urban motorways 130km/h (80mph).

Lighting
From dusk to sunrise use dipped headlights in built up areas.

Compulsory accessories
Spare bulbs for headlights, safety lock on doors, left hand driving mirror, advance warning signal (triangle).

Hooting
Between dusk and dawn use flashing headlights if it is necessary to warn other road users, only use your horn in an emergency.

Crash Helmets
Compulsory for both rider and passengers of all types of motorcycles inside and outside built up areas.

Seat belts
Compulsory everywhere and in no case may children under-10 years old sit in the front of a vehicle.

Fines
Drivers that are liable for a fine and cannot show proof of an address or of employment within French territory must pay immediately on demand; the police will provide a receipt.

Roads
France has a road network covering a total of about 930,000 miles, including 3,000 miles of motorway. Maintenance is excellent on minor 'D' roads which offer the advantage of less traffic and beautiful country.

Car hire
The CSNCRA *(Chambre Syndicate Nationale de Commerce et de la Réparation Automobile)* publishes a directory of those of its members who run a car hire service (all makes).
CSNCRA
6 rue Léonardo-de-Vinci, Paris.

By Train
The French railway network, SNCF, offers various ways of fast, inexpensive travel.
NB All rail tickets must be *'composted'* — pre-stamped before boarding train. There are *'composting'* machines at every platform entrance.
1 'France Vacances' — pass entitles unlimited travel all over France. Details from travel agents or from any French Railways office abroad.

2 'Train + Auto' — 200 stations providing a self-drive car to await your arrival. Details from the Central booking office in Paris, Tel: 292 02 92 or information leaflets from any railway station.

3 'Train Autos Couchettes, (Car sleeper trains).

4 'Train + Vélo' — service for cyclists. Over 100 stations at which a cycle for use in the town for rides in the country may be booked. See 'Train + Vélo' leaflet from travel agents or French railway stations.

Further information from:
SNCF French Railways Ltd,
179 Piccadilly, London W1X 0BA
Tel: 01 493 4451

SNCF French Railways
610 Fifth Avenue
New York, New York
Tel: 212 582 2110

By Air
Internal
AIR INTER is a prosperous
company running daily flights to 30
towns in France. An extensive
system of reduced rates for all
passengers may bring your fare
down by nearly 60%.
For all particulars: contact Air
France (Georgian House, 69 Boston
Manor Road, Brenton, Middlesex.
Tel: 01 568 4411), or your own travel
agency.
C.T.A.R. *(Comité des Transporteurs
Aériens Régionaux)* represents ten
regional air lines.
All particulars from: 15 Square
Max-Hymans, 75741 Paris Cedex
15. Tel: 5671265

There are regular flights from Paris
to Rennes, Dinard, Saint-Brieuc,
Lannion, Brest, Quimper, Lorient
and Nantes.

From the UK to the Dordogne area
London-Heathrow to Bordeaux
Two flights per day — one British
Airways and one Air France. Check
with your travel agent for details.

From the USA to the Dordogne area
TWA, Pan-Am, Air France, Air
Canada and other airlines fly to
Paris. There are connecting flights
via Air France from Paris to
Bordeaux.

ACCOMMODATION

Hotels
Hôtels de Tourisme are divided into
categories according to quality of
accommodation and standard of
service and are identified by the
number of stars.
***** L Palatial de luxe establishment
****
***
**
  * *Ordinary tourist hotel with
  adequate amenities*

Motel de Tourisme marked 'M' are
classified in accordance with the
same criteria as the hotels.

Relais de Tourisme are hotels with a
smaller number of rooms which
cater for visitors desirous of
enjoying a more elaborate cuisine.
They are marked 'R.T.'.

Les Logis de France are small or
medium hotels meeting a specific
code of requirements, generally in
the 1 and 2 star class.

Youth Hostels
There are many youth hostels in the
area.

Further details can be obtained
from:
YHA, Trevelyan House
8 St Stephen's Hill
St Albans, Herts AL1 2DY England
Tel: St Albans 55215

Fédération Unie des Auberges de
  Jeunesse
6 rue Mesnil, 751165 Paris
Telephone: 2855540

American Youth Hostels
132 Spring Street
New York, New York
Tel: 212 431 7100

WALKING AND CYCLING IN THE DORDOGNE

While this book assumes that the traveller in the Dordogne will have a car, there are plenty of footpaths and the wise traveller will not let the day pass without at least one walk. It is also possible to hire bicycles at many of the railway stations, notably at Brantôme, Bergerac, Limeuil, Périgueux and Sarlat.

LONG-DISTANCE WALKS

A number of the long-distance footpaths of the Grande Randonnée network cross the Dordogne. Visitors will see the red and white waymark slashes on their travels. The main paths are:

GR 6. From Ste Foy-la-Grande to Trémolat, 47 miles (75km)

GR 6-64, GR 6. Trémolat to Souillac, 47 miles (75km) with a diversion, GR 64, to Les Eyzies and Grotezac 12½ miles (20km)

GR 36. Sentier Normandie-Pyrénées. A section of this long path passes through the Dordogne, taking in Brantôme, Périgueux, Montignac, Biron and Montpazier; a fine walk.

GR 6-36. This is a diversion off the GR 36, 42 miles (68km) from Bonaguil in Lot, up to the *bastide* at

Villeréal, and on to Monbazillac. It can be followed in the reverse direction of course.

GR 461. A very short 12½ miles (20km) path from Montignac to Terrasson.

GR 436. A nice three-day walk of just over 43 miles (69km) from Brantôme to Pensol.

Illustrated booklets, or 'topo-guides' to these walks can be obtained in the main bookshops. Further information on local walks is obtainable from the Tourist Office in Périgueux, or from local *Syndicat d'Initiative.*

MAPS

Obtain (on arriving in the area or before) the Institut Géographique National Carte Touristique No 110 Bordelais-Périgord. Scale 1:250,000 (1km = 2.5cm).

A comprehensive lists of books is given in the bibliography and these may be obtained from your local bookshop or library.

USEFUL ADDRESSES

Further advice and information can be obtained from:
The French Government Tourist Office
178 Piccadilly, London W1V 0AL

Maison du Périgord
30 Rue Louis le Grand
75002 Paris
Tel: 010 33 (1) 742 09 15

Office Départemental de Tourisme
de la Dordogne
16 Rue President Wilson
24000 Périgueux
Tel: (53) 53 44 35

Comité Départemental de Tourisme
de la Corrèze
Quai Baluze
19000 Tulle
Tel: (55) 26 46 88

Comité Départemental de Tourisme
du Lot
Quai Cavaignac
46000 Cahors
Tel: (65) 35 07 09

Comité Départemental de Tourisme
de la Gironde

Maison du Tourisme
12 Cours du 30 Juillet
33080 Bordeaux Cedex
Tel: (56) 44 84 47

French Government Tourist Office
610 5th Avenue
New York, New York

BASTIDE TOWNS OF PARTICULAR INTEREST

Eymet
Villeréal
Monpazier
Villefranche-du-Périgord

Bibliography

Three Rivers of France,
  Freda White, (Faber & Faber, 1962)
West of the Rhône
  Freda White, (Faber & Faber)
The Hungry Archaeologist in France
  Glyn Daniel, (Faber & Faber 1962)
The Companion Guide to South-West France
  Richard Barber (Collins)
Ways of Aquitaine
  Freda White, (Faber & Faber, 1968)
The Languedoc
  George Savage, (Barrie & Jenkins)
Beyond the Dordogne
  Neil Lands, (Spurbooks)
French Leave
  Richard Binns, (Chiltern House)
Dordogne
  (Michelin Green Guide)
The Dordogne Region of France
  Ian Scargill, (David & Charles, 1974)
Dordogne
  Joy Law (Macdonald, 1981)
The Cave Artists
  Ann Sievening (Thames & Hudson, 1980)